THE DONNELLYS
a drama with music
by Peter Colley

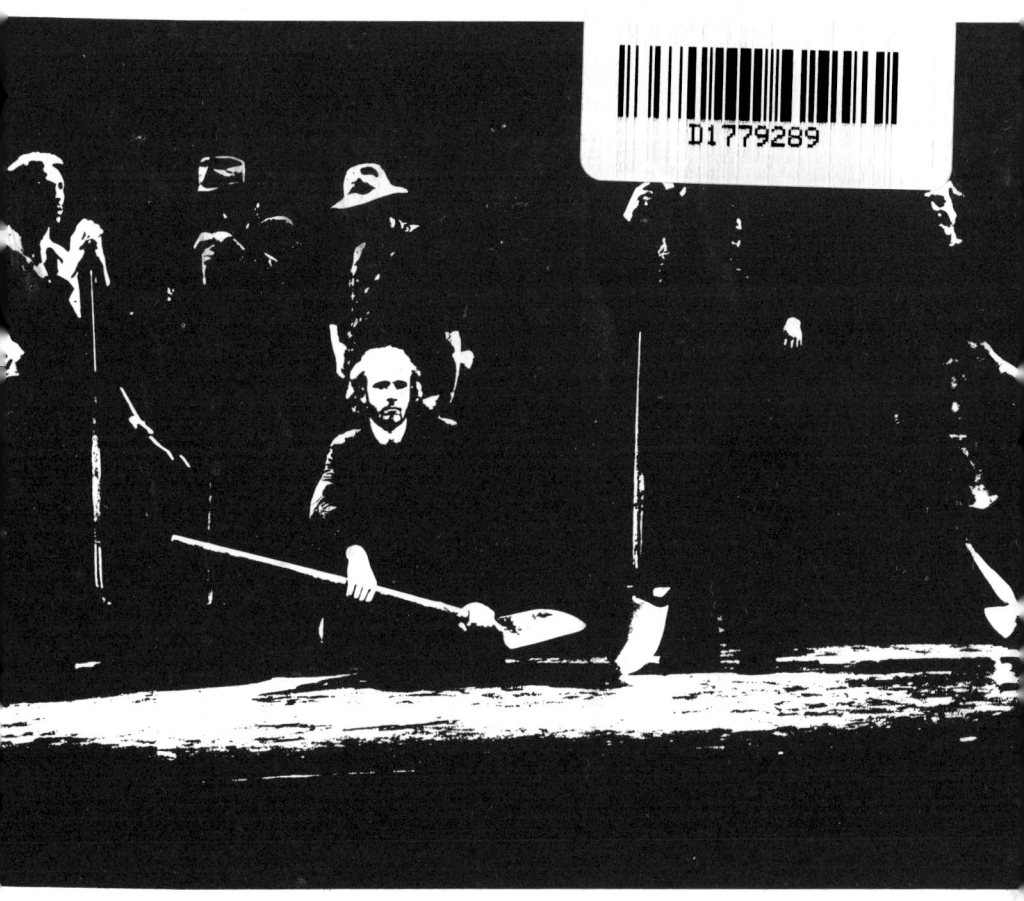

We would like to express our gratitude to The Canada Council and the Ontario Arts Council for their support.

Marian M. Wilson, Publisher

THE DONNELLYS
© Copyright 1974 by Peter Colley
All rights reserved

No part of this book may be reproduced or transmitted in any form by any means, electronic or mechanical, including photocopying and recording, information storage and retrieval systems, without permission in writing from the publisher, except by a reviewer who may quote brief passages in a review.

Professionals and amateurs are hereby warned that this play is subject to royalty, being fully protected under the copyright laws of the Dominion of Canada and the United States of America, and all countries covered by the International Copyright Union, and all countries covered by the Pan-American Copyright Convention, and the Universal Copyright Convention.

All rights, including professional, amateur, motion picture, recitation, lecturing, public reading, radio broadcasting, television, and the rights of translation into foreign languages, are strictly reserved. Particular emphasis is laid on the question of readings, permission for which must be secured in writing. **All inquiries should be addressed to the author** c/o Simon & Pierre Publishing Company Limited, P.O.Box 280 Adelaide Street Postal Station, Toronto, Ontario, Canada M5C 2J4.

Whenever the play is produced, the following notice must appear on all programs, printing and advertising for the play: "Produced by special arrangement with Simon & Pierre Publishing Company Limited" Authorship credit must be given on all programs, printing and advertising for the play.

ISBN 0-88924-058-2
1 2 3 4 5/79 78 77 76
Simon & Pierre Publishing Company Limited, Order Department
P.O.Box 280 Adelaide Street Postal Station
Toronto, Ontario, Canada M5C 2J4

Author

Peter Colley comes from England where his grandparents managed several music halls. He himself did not enter this field until he was studying for his B.A. at the University of Sheffield. At that time, he started writing, directing and acting in various comedy revues. His first play THE SAGA OF REGIN was produced at the Drama Studio, Sheffield, in 1971.

Since then, Mr. Colley has played many major roles in his career: Felix Ungar in THE ODD COUPLE, Henry Higgins in MY FAIR LADY, Sir Andrew Aguecheek in TWELFTH NIGHT, and Fagin in OLIVER, to name but a few. He also played Grouchy Ryder in the original production of THE DONNELLYS.

Coming to Canada originally as an actor with Theatre London, he wrote a short play called THE BOX which played at Theatre London's Mini-Theatre. This led to a commission to write THE DONNELLYS for Theatre London's main stage.

THE DONNELLYS turned out to be the most successful play in the theatre's seventy-year history, and many thousands were turned away at the doors. A 1976 revival ran for three weeks at the National Arts Centre in Ottawa, and also played to capacity houses in London.

Mr. Colley's next play YOU'LL GET USED TO IT . . . THE WAR SHOW opened to rave reviews in London, and later moved to a very successful run in Toronto. He also wrote Theatre London's high school touring play in 1975, and was commissioned by the University of Western Ontario to work on their 1978 University Centennial project.

Composer

Berthold Carrière, who wrote the music for THE DONNELLYS, is an experienced composer and musical director.

For three seasons at Theatre London, he was musical director for all productions. Subsequently, he became musical director for Stratford Festival's touring productions of THE TEMPEST and HAMLET. He is now Director of Music for drama at the Stratford Festival.

Among other plays, Mr. Carrière has created scores for THE IMAGINARY INVALID, ST. JOAN, DEATH OF A SALESMAN and THE DONNELLYS, and is currently writing music for a production in early 1977 at Theatre London, entitled ALICE THROUGH THE LOOKING GLASS.

Original cast
Whiteboy, Jim Toohey, Vigilante, Meredith — Greg Brandt
Tim Mulligan — Wayne Burnett
Jim Donnelly — Tom Celli
Whiteboy, Constable, Wedding Party, Grouchy Ryder — Peter Colley
Johannah Donnelly — Patricia Collins
Father Connolly, Vigilante — Robert Cooper
Gossip, Sewing Bee, Wedding Party, Vigilante — Diane Cuthbert
Settler, Barman, McLaughlin — Art Fidler
Jim Donnelly Jr., Wedding Party, Pat Quigly — Tim Grantham
Sewing Bee, Wedding Party, Mrs. Whelan, Vigilante — Caroline Guerin
Gossip, Wedding Party, Vigilante — Darcia Hiltz
Jennie Donnelly, Wedding Party — Karna Ivey
Gossip, Sewing Bee, Wedding Party, Vigilante — Alicia Jeffery
Will Donnelly — David G. Marriage
Gossip, Sewing Bee, Wedding Party, Bridget Donnelly — Shelley Matthews
Settler, Patrick Donnelly, Vigilante, Wedding Party, Johnny O'Connor — Tom McCamus
Priest, Carswell, John Donnelly, Vigilante — Rick Prevett
Gossip, Sewing Bee, Wedding Party, Vigilante — Dace Reimanis
Whiteboy, Farrell, Flanagan, Vigilante, John Purtell — Jim Schaefer
Whiteboy, Tom Donnelly, Railway Guard, Vigilante, Will Casey — Tom Stebing
Whiteboy, Settler, Bob Donnelly, Vigilante, Wedding Party, Ed Ryan — Claude R. Tessier
James Carroll — David Wallett
Irving, Judge, Michael Donnelly — David Wasse
Settler, Thomson, Wedding Party, Mike Madigan, Vigilante — Cecil Wilson

Original production
The original production of THE DONNELLYS opened in 1974 at Theatre London, London, Ontario.
Directed by Heinar Piller
Original Music Composed by Berthold Carrière
Set Designed by Antonin Dimitrov
Lighting Designed by David Wallett
Costumes Designed by Olga Dimitrov

Dedication The author, Peter Colley, wishes to dedicate this book to Heinar Piller

Play background

The memory of the Donnellys dies hard. In the many years of retelling, it has drifted into the realm of legend. In south-western Ontario, it is certainly the greatest of the folk-legends and has inspired many writers. The legend has painted the Donnellys very black indeed, although recent evidence indicates that they could not possibly have committed all the crimes of which they were accused. Since the massacre took place in 1880, it is very difficult to say what is factual and what is the product of too many bar-room raconteurs. However, this much is fact: in the early hours of February 4th, 1880, the townspeople of Lucan, Ontario rose up against the Donnelly family and murdered as many of them as they could find. That night saw the destruction of Jim and Johannah Donnelly (the parents of the seven Donnelly boys), Tom and John their sons, and their niece Bridget. After the Vigilante Committee had brutally murdered the family, it proceeded to burn the Donnelly farmstead to the ground, and even many of the bones were stolen by souvenir-hunters.

In death, the Donnellys assumed proportions which they had not even managed to attain in life, and the arguments about the justification of the killing rage on even today. We will never know for sure. This play does not claim to be the exact truth; simply a dramatic representation of the way it may have occurred, using as much of the available information as possible. In fact, some of the events and dialogue are taken directly from newspapers and court records of the time. Whichever way you look at it, however, the story of the Donnelly family will continue to intrigue writers and entertain the public for many years to come.

Additional background

Books
THE DONNELLYS MUST DIE by Orlo Miller
THE BLACK DONNELLYS (The True Story of Canada's Most Barbaric Feud) by Thomas P. Kelley
VENGEANCE OF THE BLACK DONNELLYS by Thomas P. Kelley
Article
"The Canadian Magazine", an article on the Donnellys by Frank Rasky (March 16, 1974)
Plays
THEM DONNELLYS by The Company of Theatre Passe-Muraille, originally presented in 1973
BOYS, YOU HAVE DONE ENOUGH TONIGHT by Hugh Graham, originally presented by Trent University, Peterborough, Ontario, in 1974
HANDCUFFS — THE DONNELLYS, Part 1; ST. NICHOLAS HOTEL — THE DONNELLYS, Part 2; STICKS AND STONES — THE DONNELLY Part 3 —— a trilogy by James Reaney, originally presented by the Tarragon Theatre, Toronto, Ontario, from 1973 to 1975

Cast of characters

Jim Donnelly — Father of the family. Stubborn and quick-tempered when provoked, but hard-working and reasonable most of the time.
Johannah Donnelly — Jim's wife. A very strong, practical woman. Once she makes up her mind, she forges forward with great determination. She has the strength of will to raise her large family single-handedly when necessary, and remains loyal to her husband through all his misfortunes.
Will Donnelly — Second son of Jim Donnelly. The leader of the Donnelly boys. Has a noticeable limp from a crippled foot. He is not big, but is aggressive and fairly well educated.
Tim Mulligan — Eternally drunk Irishman. Wears a tatty coat and hat. Has a small shoulder bag with bottle of whisky sticking out. Provides narration and comic relief.
Joe Carswell — Rather ostentatiously dressed landowner. Has fur trim on his jacket and sports a silver walking cane. However, rather spineless when challenged.
Pat Farrell — A thick-set Irish troublemaker. Loud and aggressive — these characteristics increase in direct relationship to the amount of alcohol he consumes.
Aemilius Irving, Q.C. — Plays all of the judges throughout the play, as well as his own character. Typical stiff representation of justice.
Martin McLaughlin — Friend of Will Donnelly. A scholarly man who is perturbed by the tough life-style of Will and his brothers. He becomes a magistrate, and is fairly easily convinced that the Donnellys are the cause of Lucan's problems.
Father Connolly — Local priest. He is naive and very quick to believe the things he is told. He is dragged into the Donnelly story rather unwittingly, and although he helped form the Vigilante Committee, it paid little heed to him.
James Carroll — A roughneck and bully. He is tough and he knows it. He is not totally without feeling, but considers himself a bit of a local hero in waging war against the Donnellys.
Toohey — Local farmer. Hates the Donnellys.
Flanagan — Owner of local stageline.
Thompson — Grumpy old man.
Jim Feeheeley — A young friend of Tom Donnelly.
Pat Quigly — A hanger-on in Carroll's gang, although he secretly befriends the Donnellys.
Purtell — An extremely slow-witted but brutal member of the Vigilante Committee.
Madigan — Member of Vigilante Committee.
Will Casey — An ex-magistrate and member of the Vigilante Committee.
Grouchy Ryder — A farmer who has become very embittered by several attacks on his property. Also partial to the bottle.

Ed Ryan — Member of the Vigilante Committee.
Elliot — A Protestant friend of Jim Donnelly.
Janet — Local lady. She is very pregnant and rather slow-witted.
Agnes — Local lady. Old and crotchety.
Dora — Local lady. Strong-minded. Doesn't believe gossip.
Annie — Local lady. Doesn't like the Donnellys, and believes everything she hears.
Johnny O'Connor — A young boy (12 years old). He was the only eye-witness to the massacre.
Bridget — Niece of the Donnellys.
Assorted — Priests, barmen, constables, Donnelly boys, reporters, street vendors.

General setting Although part of the opening action takes place in Ireland, most of the play is set in various locations in and around Lucan, Ontario.

Time Between 1844 and 1881

SACRED IN
Memory
of
HAN LYNCH WHO DE
PARTED THIS LIFE. APR
18 AD 1842. Aged 24 Years
NATIVE OF KNOCTOPHE
CO KILKENNY
Ireland

"Be always prepared to die for it
is a dreadful thing to fall into the
hands of the LIVING GOD"

WALTER BURKE
a native of the
CO TIPPERARY
who was EXECUTED
FOR THE MUTINY ON
THIS ISLAND SEP
1834 AGED 28 Yrs

Act one The play opens with a low, ominous, rumbling sound. It is the sound of a cluster of notes on a large church organ. It begins softly and builds towards a crescendo. The house lights fade, and the sound of wind is added. A picture fades into view on the screen. It is a film of a large tree standing gauntly against the sky-line of a barren, wintery field. Beside it is a man. He walks towards the camera with a pronounced limp. As he gets nearer the camera, his scarf blowing in the icy wind, an expression of deep hatred can be seen on his face. At the beginning of the film, a sad and haunting tune takes over from the sound of the wind and the organ. As the music progresses, the man's face fills the screen — finally, all that is left is the man's eyes staring accusingly at the audience. The man is William Donnelly. (If the film is not used, a slide of the Donnelly grave is shown with the figure of a man silhouetted against the screen. A spot picks out his face, and his eyes stare accusingly at the audience. The man is William Donnelly.) Suddenly, the stage lights come on to reveal the company. Everyone is in black with no distinguishing costumes.

(Mulligan enters wearing a dirty overcoat and battered hat.)

Mulligan:
Back in 1880, there was hatred in the air.
The bloody feuds of Ireland had found a foothold there.
The angry roar of horses hooves were echoing the sound.
This night we'll put the Donnellys full six feet underground.

(Slide 1 — map of Lucan and London.)

All *(sing)*:
Forty men went riding, though hundreds more knew why.
Forty men went shouting, "The Donnellys must die!"
And when the night was over and the murdering was through,
A silence came to Lucan town that death could not undo.
Come follow us one hundred years
And we'll take you back to Lucan town and the Black Donnellys.

(Slide 2 — map of Ireland and England.)

Mulligan: The curse of old Ireland, they called it.

(The following lines are done by individuals in the company.)

One: Three hundred years of hate.

Two: The beginning:

Three: Cromwell came to Ireland.

All: And there was us.

Four: Shannons,

Five: O'Haras,

Six: Kellys.

Seven: Catholics and Irish.

All: And them:

Eight: Blakes,

Nine: Walkers,

Ten: Deschamps.

Eleven: Protestants and English.

Twelve: Three hundred years of hate.

All *(sing)*:
    Hate was there in plenty and murderers two score;
    We'll never get the Donnellys on this side of the law.
    But the one they hated most of all still stands alive and tall:
    Will Donnelly by fate survives to prosecute them all.

    It's autumn now, summer's gone and justice must be done,
    But the heat of mankind's hatred won't fade beside the sun,
    And if you scream for justice, just stop and think awhile:
    How can a man of law demand to put a town on trial?

Irving: Gentlemen of the jury, you have been called here to pass judgment on one of the foulest and blackest crimes which has ever blighted the history of the Dominion — the culmination of a long and bitter feud that has made Biddulph Township a byword for lawlessness and violence. Why did the so-called "honest" citizens of Biddulph leave the comfort of their homes that cold February night, and attempt to annihilate an entire family? *(Slide 3 — a map of the*

Tipperary area) Mr. William Donnelly, your parents were Irish, were they not?

Will Donnelly: Yes, sir, they came from Tipperary.

Elliot *(to Jim Donnelly)*: That's a fine mare, Jim. But mind the Whiteboys don't find out you're selling it to a Protestant.

Jim Donnelly: The Devil take them! Those bully-boys will not be telling me who I can sell my horses to.

Whiteboy 2: Jim Donnelly was over at Elliot's yesterday. Sold him that chestnut mare.

Whiteboy 1: Elliot?

Whiteboy 2: Aye . . . a Protestant.

(Slide 4 — neutral — blue colour.)

Will Donnelly *(to Irving)*: They said we was associating with Protestants.

Irving: They?

Will Donnelly: The Whiteboys. They were a secret society in Ireland, got together to put the fear of God into the Protestant landlords . . . and any Catholics who had dealings with them.

Whiteboy 1: Sold a horse to a Protestant, eh? Maybe we should pay him a visit? Get up the rest of the boys.

(Slide 5 — the words "Tipperary 1844". Whiteboys 1 and 2 go off to the back of the set to put hats and jackets on, then join four other Whiteboys. Other members of the company set a table and chairs in centre stage. Johannah is sitting working when Jim enters with some firewood.)

Jim Donnelly: Johannah . . . I just seen lanterns coming up from the village . . . half a dozen maybe.

(Slide 6 — warm colour — red.)

Johannah: Coming our way?

Jim Donnelly: Aye . . . looks like it.

Johannah: It's a bit late for anyone to be calling. You don't think they're here about the mare?

Jim Donnelly: I don't know . . . it's possible. Well, if it's trouble they're after, I'll give them their due — and more. *(Knocking at door)* Mind your words now, Johannah. *(More knocking — Jim opens the door to several men)* Well, hello boys . . . Pat . . . Bill . . . come on in.

Men: Evening . . . Jim . . . Johannah.

Jim Donnelly: Well, now . . . it's nice to see you. How are you all? *(Mumblings of "fine" and "alright" from the group, followed by an uncomfortable silence)* Well, what can I do for you? Would you care for a jar?

Whiteboy 1: No thank you, Jim, we're on business.

Jim Donnelly: Business?

Whiteboy 1: We're after a few words with you . . . alone. *(He indicates Johannah.)*

Johannah: What's Jim's business is mine.

Whiteboy 2: Aye, but this is men's talk.

Jim Donnelly: Get on with it.

Whiteboy 2: We're not out to cause trouble, Jim. It's nothing more than some help we're after.

Whiteboy 1: There's a job needs doing for the Whiteboys.

Jim Donnelly: Then get a Whiteboy to do it.

Whiteboy 1: Well, that's what we've come about, Jim. You're Catholic. . . . You're one of us. But you've displayed a kind of . . . how would you say . . .

Whiteboy 2: Reluctance.

Whiteboy 1: Aye, that's a nice word . . . reluctance. You've displayed a kind of reluctance to join. It's not gone unnoticed.

Johannah: Just because he's not after murdering people in their beds.

Whiteboy 2: Not just people. English murderers and Protestant landlords are the ones that don't sleep easy. Which is bringing me to another point. Seems there's talk going round that you've been doing business with Protestants. Well, now, I wasn't after believing it myself. It's unheard of, I said, an honest Catholic associating with Protestant bastards. I'd shake hands with the Devil himself the day Jim Donnelly would stoop that low. Donnelly's a good man, I said, let's go ask him. *(Pause)* Well, Jim?

Jim Donnelly: I do business with a lot of people. I don't ask them all which church they go to.

Whiteboy 1: Is it true, Jim?

Jim Donnelly: How the hell should I know?

Whiteboy 1: Do you do business with Protestants?

Jim Donnelly: And what if I do?

Whiteboy 1: I want an answer, Donnelly.

Jim Donnelly: Yes, goddamn it! I do, and I'll do business with who the hell I like!

(Pause.)

Whiteboy 1: I'd rather you hadn't said that, Donnelly. *(Pause)* Well . . . I can't help you now.

(They grab Jim, and a fracas results with Johannah coming to help him, biting and scratching.)

Whiteboy 2: Get a-hold of that bastard she-bitch!

(They drag Johannah to one side where she is held by two men.)

Whiteboy 1: You're cutting your own throat, Donnelly. If you associate with scum, you become scum. Being Catholic won't save you. Remember what happened to the Nangles and the Courceys.

If you want to live in peace, you must come with us and do as you're damn well told. You're too pig-headed by half. See this, Donnelly? *(He shows him a piece of paper.)*

Jim Donnelly: What the hell's that?

Whiteboy 1: It's the Whiteboy's oath, and I want to hear you swear allegiance to it. Read him the oath.

Whiteboy 2: On your knees, and with your hand on the Good Book, you must swear:

(Slide 7 — a cold colour — dark green. The lights dim on the centre stage, and the figures placed around the set appear in silhouette. The oath is spoken in a conspiratorial whisper reinforced by tape-recorded whisperings.)

Voice: One!

All: That I will, at any hour, whether by night or day, perform without fail or inquiry such commands as my superiors may lay upon me.

Voice: Two!

All: I also declare that I will not admit or propose a Protestant or heretic as a member of our fraternal society, knowing him to be such.

Voice: Three!

All: That I will always give preference in dealing to those who are attached to our national cause, and that I will not deal with a Protestant or heretic — so long as I can deal with one of my own faith on equal terms.

Voice: Four!

All: That I will not give evidence in any court of law or justice against a brother, but aid him in his defence by any means in my power.

(Lights change back. Slide 8 — warm colour — red.)

Whiteboy 1: Get on your knees, Donnelly, and swear.

Jim Donnelly: I will not.

(Silence.)

Whiteboy 1: You've had this coming for a long while.

(They beat him up, and leave him on the floor.)

Johannah: You cowardly bastards! You're like a pack of rats.

Whiteboy 1: You must come with us, Donnelly. Come with us, or we'll call you Blackfoot.

Jim Donnelly: Call me what you like!

Whiteboy 1: You're a fool. You're doing the same as Walker did. You remember Walker?

Whiteboy 3: He had dealings with the English tyrants. He's dead now, but before he died he took a bath in a barrel of thorns.

Whiteboy 2: And had his lying tongue cut out.

Whiteboy 1: Remember, Donnelly?

Jim Donnelly: Get out. Get out of here.

Whiteboy 1: Alright, leave him alone. *(He motions to the others, and they draw back)* Look around you, Donnelly. See the eyes that are watching you? Recognize what you see? That's hate you're looking at. You'll be seeing that look again, because you're a Blackfoot, and it'll follow you as sure as your own shadow. And no matter how far you run, you'll have to keep looking over your shoulder — and eyes like these will be watching you, until one night you'll pay your debt in blood. Remember, Donnelly, Ireland never forgets its enemies.

(They leave. Jim and Johannah look at each other in silence. The mood is reinforced by a music bridge.)

Johannah: Did they hurt you bad?

Jim Donnelly: Those bastards don't frighten me. I could beat the hide off any of them.

Johannah: There's too many of them, Jim. You can't be fighting them all. We're best out of all this.

Jim Donnelly: What, and have it said that I ran away? I'd never give them the satisfaction.

Johannah: You know how often we've talked about Canada. In Canada there's farmland . . . a future, and a chance to do something with it. What have we got here? We'll never be able to have our own land. The potato crops have failed for the last two years, and now there's talk of another rebellion. There'll be another blood bath like the '98. The old-timers are shaking their heads because they remember, but the young ones don't listen to them any more. God, how soon they forget the senselessness of it all! Can't you see, Jim, even without the Whiteboys, we've got a dog's chance in hell.

Jim Donnelly: Damn your eyes, Johannah, but I know you're right. *(Pause)* And being right's a man's job, so keep your mouth shut. *(He moves thoughtfully and sits down)* How would you like to go to Canada?

Johannah: Canada?

Jim Donnelly: Aye, Canada.

Johannah: Seems like a good idea.

Jim Donnelly: Good? It's a great idea. I'm glad I thought of it.

(Slide 9 — collage of ship's sails and masts. The musical introduction to the sea-crossing song begins as the slide of a ship's sails appears on the screen. As the members of the company sing, they circle the set, picking up luggage and putting on costumes as they go, making their way to the central playing area which becomes the deck of a ship.)

All *(sing)*:
    Today we shall ride
    On a bright Irish tide,
    And bid fond farewells to the blarney,
    Where Orange and Green
    Are no longer seen,
    A place where no landlords can harm ye.

This is the story that always is told
By all who would come to the land of the bold.
Whether Cornish or Nordic, whether English or Swiss,
If Canada's bad, it's much better than this.

(The deck is full of people watching the harbour as the ship pulls away. Among them are Jim and Johannah, Johannah holding a baby in her arms, and Tim Mulligan, an old and continually drunk Irishman.)

Mulligan: Farewell, Ireland! Farewell, me dear old country. Bugger you, Ireland! What do you think I'm leaving for?

Priest: Mr. Mulligan, are you drinking?

Mulligan: I'm not drinking. I'm drunk.

Man 2 *(sings)*:
A storm came and blew
For a good week or two,
And the women and kids were all crying.
Ship's fever was rife
To add to our strife
And many a man was near dying.

Priest: . . . And may the Lord accept the souls of these humble people, whose dreams ended before they had a chance to begin.

Man 1: There's another one down with cholera. That's sixty in all.

Man 2: The lookout then cried
That land he espied.
And for joy all the lassies were weeping.

Lookout: Land ho!

Priest *(spoken over music)*: Look at this beautiful land, my friends. This will be our heaven on earth.

Mulligan *(drunk again — looks out)*: So this is our heaven? *(Doesn't like what he sees)* Bloody hell!

All *(sing)*:
This is the story that always is told
By all who would come to the land of the bold.

Whether Cornish or Nordic, of low rank or birth,
The sea don't compare with a nice piece of earth.

At Grosse Isle we stopped
And anchor was dropped,
Then we took to the river for Kingston.
From there down to York
On a ship like a cork,
Where we left for a town they call London.

(Slide 10 — London in the 1840's.)

Mulligan: Bit of a nerve calling this London. There's bugger all here. What's this . . . Ridout Street. Nothing. York Street . . . aha! McGregor's Tavern! I feel at home already. *(He stumbles off.)*

All *(sing)*:
This is the story that always is told
By all who would come to the land of the bold.
Whether wildwood or forest, there's nothing so grand
In all of God's heaven as your own piece of land.

(By now, the ship has been rearranged to show people waiting at a stagecoach station, with Jim and Johannah sitting on their luggage, looking rather tired.)

Jim Donnelly: A piece of land. That's what we need. We're farm people . . . there's nothing for us in London.

Johannah: Get a job for a while . . . just until we get up the money. It's not a bad wage clearing the land.

Jim Donnelly: What . . . come all the way to Canada and then end up clearing someone else's land. I'm not working for another landlord, and that's final! *(Changes his mood)* I hear there's plenty of land up in the Queen's bush around Biddulph Township. It's scarce fourteen miles north on the Proof Line.

Johannah: Who'll be owning it?

Jim Donnelly: Absentee landlords. If you clear the land, you can lay claim to it. Squatter's rights, they call it.

Johannah: Jim, what if someone brings the law in?

Jim Donnelly: Aah . . . the owner probably doesn't live within a hundred miles, and even if he does, what the hell . . . it's not right for a man to have land and not use it. Yup . . . I reckon that's what we'll do. *(Slide 11 — open sky and clouds. The music starts, and Jim and Johannah pick up their luggage while the company forms a long procession. As a line of immigrants loaded with their belongings, they circle the stage, each group finding a piece of land and exiting, until Jim and Johannah are left. They find some land they like and stop. Several men appear around them and close in, as an inquisitive crowd with some newcomers. There is some tension in the air)* I was wondering if you knew who'd be owning this land?

Man 1: That's Joe Carswell's land, but he never uses it. He's got a plot on the other side of the township.

Jim Donnelly: That's good land. It should be cleared.

Man 2: Go see Mr. Carswell. He'll likely sell it to you.

Jim Donnelly: Yeah . . . I may do that. I'm Jim Donnelly, this is my wife Johannah. *(They touch their hats to her)* We're from County Tipperary.

Man 4: Tipperary! Well, I'll be . . . .

Man 3: You'll really be at home here. Half of Lucan's from Tipperary.

Man 1: Donnelly, eh? Would I be right in supposing you're . . . er . . . Catholic?

Jim Donnelly: That's right.

Man 1: Well, now, that's even better. There's too many bloody Protestants here, anyway.

Man 3: Yes, you'll be really at home here, all right. When Jim Hodgins settled the township some ten years back, he brought Protestants, Catholics and bastard Blackfeet with him . . . and then he wonders why everyone's fighting.

Jim Donnelly: Fighting . . . eh?

Man 2: If you're planning to stay, mind who you neighbour with. Just down the Roman line, there's Keefes and Feeheeleys. Bad sorts.

I'd give 'em a wide berth, if I were you.

Man 4: I've heard of the Donnellys before. You weren't Whiteboys, by any chance?

Jim Donnelly: No.

Man 4: Oh. *(Pause)* It must have been someone else. Yeah . . . . Good day to you both.

(They all say, "good day" and exit, a few of them casting suspicious looks back at the Donnellys.)

Johannah: Jim, you don't think they'll find out?

Jim Donnelly: We're thousands of miles from Tipperary. We'll be alright.

Johannah: I've a feeling we're a lot closer than you think. Can't we find somewhere else?

Jim Donnelly: We've been travelling for over four months, and here's a fine piece of land. I'm a farmer, not a gypsy. Come on, let's get to work.

(The company enters with axes, spades, hammers, spinning wheels, butter churns, and mimes various activities, such as digging and knocking in fence posts. This is done during the song. Slide 12 — sunset.)

All *(sing)*:
    Hewing and chopping and pulling a plough,
    Digging and sowing and milking cows,
    We'll clear this land, though God knows how,
    Way down in Lucan town.

    There's stumps to be pulled and trees to be burned,
    Barns to be built and earth to be turned.
    If we clear this land, it'll sure be earned,
    Way down in Lucan town.

(The company ends in a frozen tableau, with Jim Donnelly sitting centre stage sharpening an axe. Mulligan sits on the side of the stage and casually addresses the audience.)

Mulligan: Well, that's how it all began, near as I can say. Mind you, I could have told them trouble was coming, but, of course, nobody bothered to ask. Not that them Donnellys were particularly bad folk — well, no more than any of those farmers were, and believe me, there are no saints in this little tale — but I had the feeling trouble would follow them around. I mean, stealing someone's land . . . it's not the best way to start. I remember when Carswell found out. *(He laughs)* He wasn't over pleased, I can tell you. He was a funny little man — wouldn't say "boo" to a goose ordinarily, but when he heard about having squatters on his land, he got madder than a hornet, and not knowing what sort of man Jim Donnelly was, he went stomping across in a mighty rage.

(Jim is working as Carswell enters.)

Carswell: Are you Jim Donnelly? Eh? Are you the guy who's squatting on my land?

Jim Donnelly *(stands and absolutely dwarfs him)*: Yup!

Carswell *(his nerve giving way)*: Oh . . . well . . . did you know that this was my land?

Jim Donnelly: Yup!

Carswell: Oh . . . did you not think that I . . . er . . . may . . . er . . . need it?

Jim Donnelly: No.

Carswell: Oh . . . ! Well, I do.

Jim Donnelly: What for?

Carswell: I beg your pardon?

Jim Donnelly: What do you need it for? You've got a plot of land already, and you've not even begun to clear this one. Doesn't look to me as though you need it.

Carswell: Now, look here, this is my land. It doesn't matter whether I need it. It's mine . . . I own it.

Jim Donnelly: Well, I'm here and I ain't moving. What are you going to do about it?

Carswell: I'm afraid you have no alternative but to buy the land, and I couldn't possibly part with it for less than $200.

Jim Donnelly *(angrily)*: What?

Carswell *(frightened)*: What am I saying? $150.

Jim Donnelly *(grabs him)*: Look, Carswell . . . .

Carswell: $140?

Jim Donnelly: Get this into your stupid head . . . .

Carswell: $135?

Jim Donnelly: I'm not moving off this land!

Carswell: $120?

Jim Donnelly: And I'm not buying it!

Carswell: $100? *(Jim releases him – pause)* $90?

Jim Donnelly: No!

Carswell: I know you're intimidating me to try and make me lower my price, but it won't work. I won't go a penny below $85. *(Jim grabs him by the collar again)* . . . 80 – 76 – 75 – 70 – 69.50? *(Chokes.)*

Jim Donnelly *(still holding him)*: I'll make an arrangement with you. As soon as I earn enough money, I'll pay you for the land. Alright?

Carswell: Never! *(Jim squeezes his throat)* Yes . . . yes . . . good idea!

Jim Donnelly: And you know what'll happen to you if you go running to the law. We understand each other?

Carswell: Yes . . . yes.

Jim Donnelly: Now, get out of here.

(Carswell exits.)

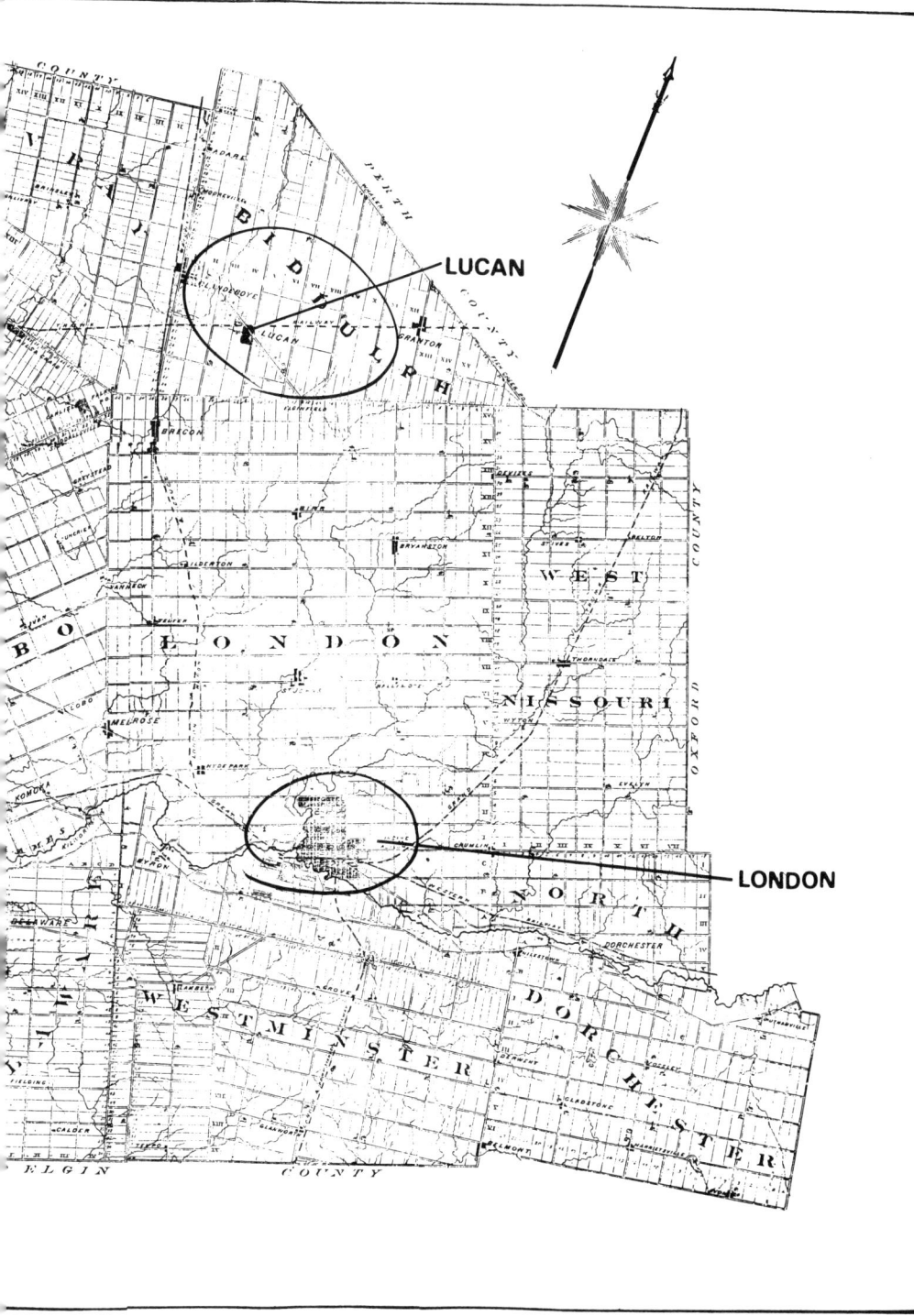

(Historical map of 1877)

Mulligan: So Carswell and Donnelly came to an "arrangement" over the land, and quite a few years passed while Jim cleared the land and raised a big family. And it may all have ended there, but for a man called Pat Farrell.

(Pat Farrell enters. He watches as the company sings the first verse while setting up a bar scene. Slide 13 — lantern.)

All *(sing)*:
>Hewing and chopping and pulling a plough,
>Digging and sowing and milking cows,
>We'll clear this land, though God knows how,
>Way down in Lucan town.

(The mood changes during the second verse, as Farrell moves toward centre stage. Donnelly and Farrell eye each other ominously.)

>Months are going, going by,
>Wheat is growing, growing high,
>But someone soon is going to die,
>Way down in Lucan town.

Farrell *(breaks the mood)*: The drinks are on me, boys!

(Suddenly the bar is filled with noise and music.)

Catholic 1: Right, lads, I'm going to sing a song.

Mulligan: Why . . . what have we done to you?

Catholic 1: Less of your lip, Mulligan.

Protestant 1: You can't sing.

Catholic 1: Sure I can bloody sing!

Protestant 1: Someone put birdseed in your beer? Come on, then, what are you going to sing?

Catholic 1: "The Wearing o' the Green."

Protestant 1: That's a damned Catholic song.

Catholic 1: So what, shithead!

Protestant 1: I'll show you so bloody what!

(As Protestant 1 goes for Catholic 1, Farrell steps in on the side of The Catholic. The Protestant 1 stops. Mulligan, not having seen this, rants on.)

Mulligan: A fight! Get 'em, boys! A left poke in the ribs, a right kick to the balls, and you're away!

(Farrell picks up Mulligan.)

Farrell: Would you be after a fight, you stinking Protestant?

Mulligan: Oh no . . . I love the Pope, I love him. *(Farrell puts him down)* It's Catholics I can't stand. *(He dashes out of Farrell's reach.)*

Farrell: You'd better keep out of my way, Mulligan. *(They settle down for a moment. Carswell enters)* Well, if it isn't Mr. Carswell. Let me buy you a drink.

Carswell: Thank you, Pat, but . . . .

Farrell: An ale for Mr. Carswell, Jack. I've been wanting to talk to you. Word's going round you've got a Blackfoot squatting on your land.

Carswell: A Blackfoot? Oh, you mean Mr. Donnelly?

Farrell: They say he just marched in without so much as a "by your leave". Now that's Black Irish for you.

Carswell: Black Irish?

Farrell: Blackfoot, Mr. Carswell. A treacherous lot. You'll never get him off the land, you know.

Carswell: But we've come to an arrangement. He says he'll buy it, when he gets the money.

Farrell: Buy it! Mr. Carswell, you know damned well he'll never buy that land.

Carswell: But he refuses to leave. What can I do?

Farrell: Sell the land.

Carswell: Sell the land? But who'd buy land with squatters on it?

Farrell: Someone who doesn't give a tinker's damn about that blowhard Donnelly.

Protestant 1: Hey, listen to that. Farrell reckons he can get Jim Donnelly off Carswell's land!

Farrell: I could beat him — and a dozen like him.

Protestant 1: I'd like to be there to see it.

Farrell: You'll see it soon enough. What about it, Mr. Carswell?

Carswell: I'd gladly sell it to you, but do you really think you can get them off the land?

Farrell: Just leave that to me. There's not a Blackfoot this side of hell would stay on that land after I'm finished with him.

Carswell: Well, if you're really serious, the land is yours — and I wish you the best of luck.

Barman: Alright, gentlemen. Time, please.

Mulligan: But, I've only just started!

Barman: That's your lot, boys.

Mulligan: I ain't moving. I'm staying here 'til I get drunk. Call this stuff whisky? I drank stronger stuff from my mother's breast.

Catholic 2: I wouldn't take that, Jack. *(To barman)* Why don't you chuck him out?

Mulligan: I'd like to see you try. *(The barman casually picks him up and throws him out. Mulligan gets up, drunkenly trying to regain his dignity)* To hell with you! I've been thrown out of better bars than this. *(Slide 14 — night sky, moon and clouds. The company laughs at him and exits, striking the set for the bar. Mulligan is left alone on stage. He exits singing)*
  Four-and-twenty virgins went up to Inverness,

> And when the ball was over there were four-and-twenty less,
> Singing balls to your partner . . . .

(Fade out. The next part of the song has a sombre and ominous quality. During it, Farrell enters and surveys the scene for a moment)

> Months are going, going by,
> Hate is growing, growing high.
> And someone soon is going to die,
> Way down in Lucan town.

(At the end of the song, Farrell walks across the stage and bangs on the ground with his foot. Slide 15 — sunset. Jim Donnelly enters.)

Farrell: Jim Donnelly?

Jim Donnelly: Yeah. And who might you be?

Farrell: The name's Pat Farrell.

Jim Donnelly: Good day to you, Mr. Farrell. What business do you have with me?

Farrell: I've come to inform you that you're trespassing.

Jim Donnelly: Well, I reckon you'd just better go back and check your information, mister.

Farrell: There's nothing wrong with my information. You don't own this land.

Jim Donnelly: That's right, I don't, but I've got an arrangement with Mr. Carswell . . . .

Farrell: But none with me. I'm the owner of this land, Donnelly.

Jim Donnelly: Now look here, mister whatever-your-name-is. I don't know what little game you think you're playing, but Mr. Carswell is the owner of this land, and I've got first option on buying it.

Farrell: Like to see the deeds, Donnelly? Nice and legal.

(Jim takes the documents and looks at them.)

Jim Donnelly: I ain't too good at reading. I'm thinking this is some kind of trick.

Farrell: You'll find out soon enough. I want you off this land, and soon. It's the law . . . .

(Enter Johannah.)

Johannah: What's up, Jim?

Jim Donnelly: This son-of-a-bitch says he owns this land.

Farrell: I've come to inform you and your family that you're trespassing on my land.

Jim Donnelly: He says he's bought this land from Carswell.

Farrell: You haven't got a leg to stand on, Donnelly! I want you off this land in ten days.

Jim Donnelly: Ten days . . . ! You think I'd leave a piece of land in ten days that took me ten years to clear? See across to those trees, and back to that barn? Good open land. When we got here, it was forest, and every tree and stump I cleared with my own hands. My hands got mighty strong clearing this land. Strong enough to break your goddamned neck, Farrell!

Farrell: Fine talk for a Blackfoot, Donnelly.

Johannah: You're going to wish that you never said that, mister!

Jim Donnelly: Fetch the kids, Johannah. I want them to see what happens to anyone who calls us Blackfeet.

Johannah *(calls offstage)*: Boys . . . come and see your father have some fun.

(The boys and Mulligan enter with adlibs such as —)

Will Donnelly: Hey . . . Dad's going to beat the piss out of someone!

(A short but ferocious fight ensues in which Jim gets the better of Farrell and knocks him down. As Farrell staggers away, he shouts obscenities at Jim.)

The Village of Lucan

...as incorporated as a village in 1872, when Robert H. O'Neil was elected Reeve, and D. McRobert, William Porte, H. B. Quarry, and A. Goodacre, Councillors. S. C. Hersey is Clerk of the village.

In 1873, R. H. O'Neil was re-elected Reeve; in 1874, Thomas Dwight, and since then, H. H Hutchins. The population is about 1,100, and the assessed value, $148,230.

Lucan was at first called Marystown, but when a post-office was opened here, about fifteen years ago, it was called Lucan. Among the first inhabitants were R. H. O'Neil, B. Stanley, William Stanley, Robert McLean, William Porte (now postmaster), M. Connigan, Robert Fox, and John Farr.

Lucan was a place of very little importance until the Grand Trunk Railway was opened, since which time its growth has been extremely rapid, and its increase in wealth wonderful. It is neat and substantial in appearance, being built mostly of white brick, and contains, besides many mercantile establishments, two steam grist-mills, a flax scutching mill, foundry and saw mill.

The energy and enterprise displayed by the inhabitants of Lucan have earned for it the high degree of prosperity which it enjoys. The welfare of the place has of late been imperilled by the unfortunate exhibitions of malice, which have lately culminated in incendiary fires, which have created a great deal of distrust, and checked for a time the progress of the village.

(Historical synopsis circa 1878)

Farrell: Make the most of it, Donnelly. You won't laugh so loud in the law courts.

(The Donnelly boys jeer at him. A spot falls on a judge on a higher level. The Donnellys and Farrell turn to listen.)

Judge: The case of Farrell versus Donnelly in the matter of Lot 18 of the 6th Concession of the Huron Tract. The bench has decided to award twenty-five acres to James Donnelly and twenty-five acres to Patrick Farrell.

(Judge exits.)

Farrell: Damnation!

Jim Donnelly: It could have been worse.

Johannah: The front field looks so narrow now. It's good land that was nothing but wild woods a few years back. It was our sweat that gave the soil its life. What Farrell did was nothing but a cheap trick.

Jim Donnelly: What's done is done. We can't change it.

Farrell: Donnelly, you haven't heard the last of this.

(Slide 16 — inside of a barn wall. The band strikes up a lively jig led by a fiddler. Part of the company dances and the other stands around drinking and talking. Two factions become apparent, each centred around Pat Farrell and Jim Donnelly. The music ends and the dancers settle for a moment.)

Mulligan: Pat Farrell had a big mouth, and it didn't take long for all of Lucan to know he would have used Jim's guts for garters. Everyone knew it was just a matter of time.

(Farrell is drunk and surrounded by several men, also drinking.)

Farrell: The only reason he put me down was because I never expected a Blackfoot to have the guts to fight. The next time, boys . . . .

Mulligan: Well, the next time was a barn-raising bee one Saturday night. No one thought it would turn out the way it did, but even though I'd had a belly full of whisky, I knew it was the beginning of the end. *(Getting drunker)* Well, really it was the end of the beginning, or around the middle of the beginning of the end . . . but still pretty close to the start of the middle of the beginning, in fact . . . I ought to shut up. Give us a tune, will you?

(The fiddler breaks into a tune and everyone starts dancing again. But, it soon becomes obvious that Farrell is spoiling for a fight, and Jim is trying to control his anger.)

Farrell: Are my eyes deceiving me, Davey, or does that man look uncommon like a thief?

Man 1: How's that?

Farrell: I said, that man's got an evil look in his eye. It's the look of a Blackfoot land-thief, if I'm not mistaken.

Man 1: Come on, Pat . . . you've had enough of that whisky.

(Farrell pushes him away angrily.)

Johannah: Take no notice of him, Jim. He's drunk and sore about you getting half the land.

Jim Donnelly: I've been listening to that big mouth for over an hour. If he carries on much longer, I'll fix it so he can't speak for a month.

Johannah: You've drunk too much yourself, Jim, so there's no point in fighting.

Farrell: Hey, Jack, I hear you got some bad weeds on your land.

Man 2 *(still dancing)*: Sure, Pat, but I cut them down.

Farrell: Well, I got weeds on my land. I got twenty-five acres with weeds all over it. You reckon I should cut them down, Jack?

Man 2: I reckon you oughta stop grousing and have a good time.

Farrell: Ah, you bastards wouldn't feel so good if you'd been robbed of your land by a sneak thief.

Jim Donnelly: Just one more crack, Farrell, and you'd better be ready to answer for it.

Farrell: Go to hell, Donnelly! *(They go for each other, but their friends grab them. The fiddle player falters momentarily, but then starts to play even louder. Jim and Farrell are brought back to their respective areas. The company dances another gay jig. Jim turns his back on Farrell. At first Farrell remains silent, but as the dance progresses he becomes increasingly argumentative, although his friends try to calm him down. Eventually he shouts at them, although obviously loud enough for Jim to hear)* What the hell do you care? No bastard Blackfoot has stolen your land!

(Jim's patience is exhausted. He slams his jug down and turns on Farrell. For a moment there is a deathly silence, Then comes the low rumbling of a cluster of organ notes similar to that heard at the beginning of the play. It will build in volume throughout the rest of the fight.)

Jim Donnelly: All right, Farrell. I'll whip you to the edge of the grave for that!

(Farrell has an axe which he throws at Jim. It misses. They begin to fight, although they are obviously too drunk to fight well.)

Woman 1: Drag them apart or they'll kill themselves!

Woman 2: They're too drunk to hurt each other. Let them be.

Woman 3: They were spoiling for a fight. Let them get it over with.

(Jim gets knocked flat after quite a struggle. Near his hand is a handspike. Farrell rushes towards him. Jim poises to hit Farrell with the handspike. Everybody freezes. The organ sound stops dead. The lights on the main scene turn deep red as a light comes up on a higher level to reveal Johannah. Slide 17 — Farrell's face showing an expression of terror as he sees the handspike about to hit him.)

Johannah: It was morning again. A single bird was singing, unseen. The early sun threw a handful of diamonds on the wet grass, and blood on the clouds at the edge of the day. Farrell's blood. *(Slide 18 — Farrell is hit. He grasps his head in his hands. Jim hits Farrell and, at the same moment, the crowd closes in. The effect is like stopping and starting a movie, but the movement only lasts about one second, then everyone freezes in a new pose)* He'd remember that dream, that same dream frozen cold. A handspike frozen in his fist, a white finger pointing into the darkness. Now, it was pointing at him. *(Slide 19 — Farrell is still holding his head, but blood is oozing down his face. Jim drops the handspike and, seeing what he has done, runs away. Again the crowd moves in closer and freezes)* We want you, Donnelly. We want you. The dew won't wash the blood away. *(Slide 20 — Farrell's face and hands are a mass of blood. Farrell falls to the floor, the crowd moves closer, and Jim runs up towards a higher level. All freeze)* Second spring. The sheets are cold beside me as I lie in bed, watching the cool brightness of the dawn dapple the walls. Somewhere, Jim is hiding and dreaming. *(Slide 21 — Farrell's body lying on the floor. The crowd closes in again. Jim reaches a place up on a higher level and stops. Everyone freezes again)* Seeing Farrell's blood in the morning sky. It'll be two years soon. That's a long nightmare, Jim. A long time to be running.

Jim Donnelly: I keep waking up like it just happened.

Johannah: The linen gently folded like a sea of snow.

Man 1: Farrell's dead!

(The crowd moves slowly back from the body. Some take the body off, the rest form little groups around the stage. There is a music bridge. A single light comes up on a constable. Slide 22 — a dark colour — blue.)

Constable: He then ran away from the scene of the crime, m'Lord, and we have not as yet managed to apprehend him.

Jim Donnelly: God, how the damp gets in your bones. I pray for the morning and the sun to drive out the damp and the dreams. Sometimes it's a grey cloudy day with a fine rain hanging in the air. Those are the worst. I'll crawl towards a barn and hide there for a while. But not too long . . . got to keep moving.

Johannah: On cold nights when there's a strong wind blowing and driving the rain, I'll look into the black outside and wonder where you are. Suddenly, a flash of lightning silhouettes the trees at the end of the far field. Is that where you're hiding tonight? I'll put three candles in the window. There's no one here except your children, Jim. The law will not be out on a night like this. *(Sound of thunder)* The summer of '57 quickly lost itself in the fall, and the winter cooled the air of the murder. So, during the cold weather, Jim slept in the barn most of the time. The months were going so slow that I scarce believed it when another summer had passed.

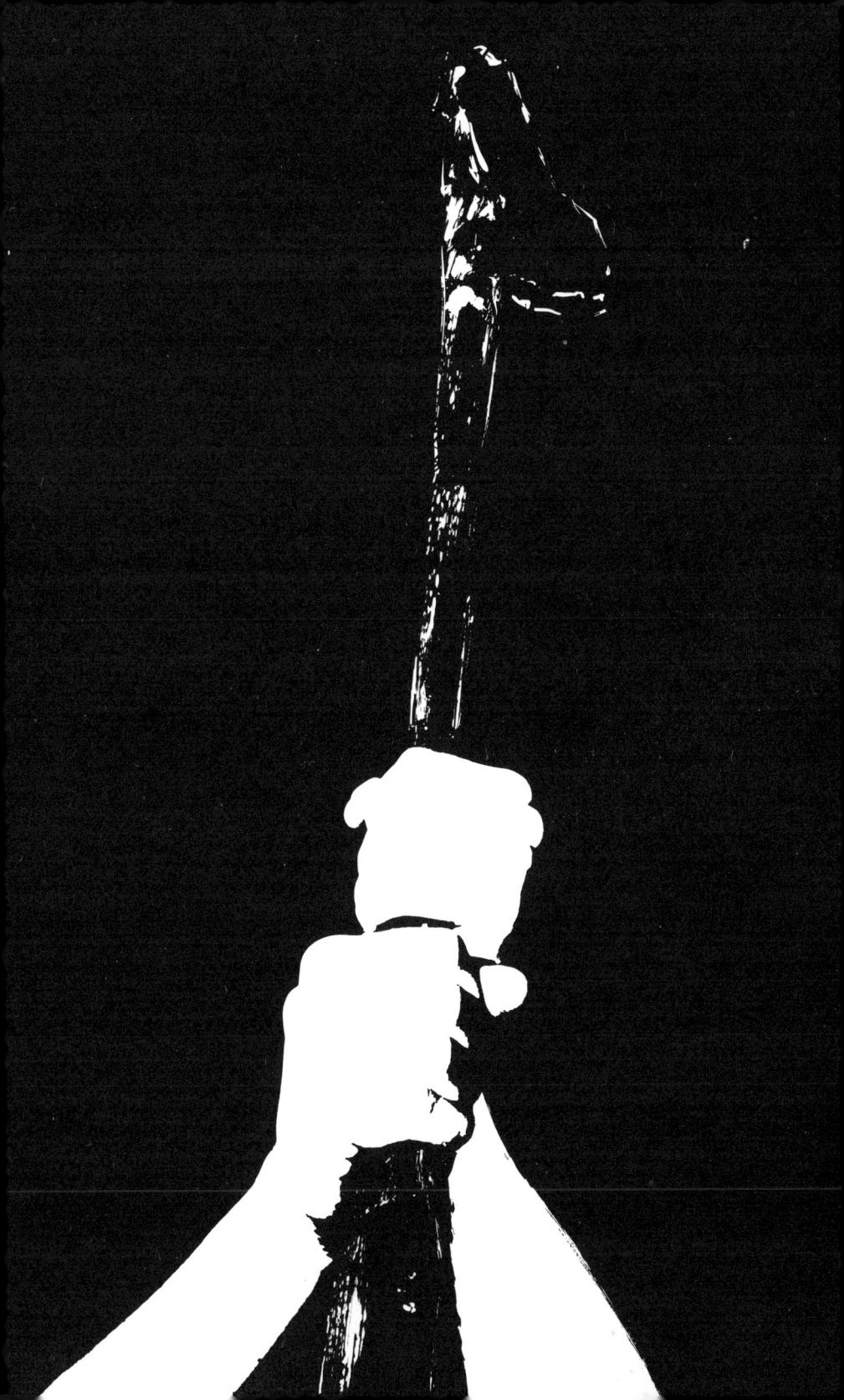

(The cast stands haphazardly on stage, while Jim and the constable play a bizarre game of hide-and-seek amongst them.)

Woman 1: Constable! I saw Jim Donnelly down by the swamp.

(The constable moves and Jim takes up another position.)

Man 1: He'll be in his barn tonight. Watch the candles she puts in the window.

(Hide-and-seek again.)

Constable: Come on, Donnelly. Give yourself up.

Woman 2: He's still around, constable. Johannah's had a baby . . . and a girl this time, thank the Lord.

Constable: Where is he, Mrs. Donnelly?

Johannah: I don't know.

Constable: I suppose that child was a divine conception, then?

Johannah: Did your ma never tell you, constable, but it takes a while for the calf to drop. It's nine months since I've seen him.

Constable: Damn your impertinence! He'll get more than nine months when I find him.

Woman 3: Constable! Over by the trees . . . look!

(The constable moves, but Jim dodges him.)

Constable: Why is it there's not a Protestant in town ever sets eyes on him . . . only Catholics. I thought he was Catholic as well.

Woman 4: Aye . . . a Black one. Watch the shadows, constable.

(The constable thinks he sees him, but Jim dodges again.)

Constable: Winter will be here soon, Donnelly. They say you're black against the snow. *(Pause)* I can wait. *(He rests.)*

Jim Donnelly: It's my second winter, and the cold is deeper than

before. Farrell's body is not half so cold as mine. He's got six feet of earth and a coffin to keep him warm. How many times have I cursed that headful of whisky fumes?

(Johannah looks at him. They have been far apart on the stage. They move towards each other . . . meeting in the centre of the highest level.)

Johannah: You can't go on running forever, Jim.

(They embrace, then Jim walks slowly toward the constable. The actors form a line past which Jim must walk. They watch him with hatred.)

Man 1: A man is walking.

Man 2: Walking down the Roman line.

Man 3: A man with blood on his hands.

Man 4: The first blood was yours, Donnelly . . . the last will be ours.

Woman 1: Jim Donnelly's walking into town.

Woman 2: Two years tiredness lines his face.

Woman 3: Two years in fields and woods.

Woman 4: For two years we have waited. Two long years. Look over your shoulder, Donnelly . . . look into our eyes. Recognize what you see?

(At the end of the line, the constable waits for him. Jim puts his hands out, and the constable puts the handcuffs on him.)

Mulligan: And that, as they say, was that. They'd got him well and truly by the short and curlies. And I saw the whole thing, as I'd been into town for a quick drink and was having a rest in my favorite gutter when it happened. Oh boy . . . I thought to myself. There's gonna be some fun now.

(A single voice sings while the company regroups.)

Voice: They took away Jim Donnelly to face a murder trial.

For the killing of Pat Farrell he'll be jailed for quite a while.
Though sudden death in a drunken brawl is not a murder true,
The Catholic men of Lucan town know well what they must do.

(A judge enters.)

Judge: Will the foreman of the jury please stand? *(Man 2 stands up)* How do you find the defendant on the charge of murder?

Man 2: Guilty, m'Lord.

Judge: James Donnelly of the Township of Biddulph, you have been found guilty of the murder of Patrick Farrell on the 27th day of June, eighteen hundred and fifty-seven. *(He puts on a black patch and a murmur of disbelief runs through the crowd)* It is the verdict of this court that you be taken from here to the jail at Goderich in the County of Huron, there to be hanged by the neck until death. And may the Lord have mercy on your soul.

(Johannah turns and faces upstage. The company speaks in unison. The constable takes Jim Donnelly away.)

All: Take Donnelly and hang him by the neck 'til he is dead.
For taking Farrell's life away, we'll see your body bled.
So you've a wife and children, all needing to be fed,
You should have thought of that before you struck Pat Farrell dead.

(They turn their backs on the audience. Johannah turns forward.)

Johannah: Jim! Jim! *(Pause)* There was nothing left but silence, and then, slowly, came the intrusion of sounds. Far away at the end of a tunnel. The distant echo of voices saying things I couldn't hear. Murmurs of people growing loud and then soft, and all I could think about was Jim. Oh my God, oh my God . . . they're taking him away. They'll steal the breath from his body and throw him into the cold ground. To be hanged by the neck until death. The words run through me, my bones freeze as brittle as chalk and there is nowhere to hide. Nowhere to hide. *(She keeps repeating this as her children approach her from a distance. Slide 23 — gallows)* No!

Will Donnelly: Are you alright, mother?

Johannah: It's not over yet, boys. We'll fight this . . . we'll keep fighting right until they pull the trap. If there's the smallest chance of saving him, we'll take it. We'll get up a petition . . . yes . . . we'll get a petition pleading for clemency . . . I'll take it to the Governor General . . . he's coming to Goderich soon . . . and we'll win . . . we'll win. God give me strength.

(The actors fill the stage, standing motionless while Johannah goes to them with a long scroll. Some sign it, others turn their backs on her and exit. William speaks from a separate area.)

Will Donnelly: I'll never forget that petition. I was thirteen at the time. Mother worked so hard, she was out from sun-up to sundown. She knocked on every farmhouse and store her tired feet could find.

Johannah: The killing was an accident.

Will Donnelly: She stopped people on the roads and in the fields.

Johannah: It was manslaughter, not murder.

Will Donnelly: Some signed, some didn't.

Johannah: I've seven boys and a baby girl need feeding.

Will Donnelly: But, the execution was getting closer, and still she didn't think the list was long enough.

Johannah: Farrell threw the axe at him first. It was self-defence.

Will Donnelly: So one Sunday, she put us in our best clothes, scrubbed our ragamuffin faces, and stood us outside the church.

Johannah: Will you sign this, please?

Will Donnelly: There was Jim, my elder brother who was seventeen, and me, John, Pat, Michael, Bob and Tom. Tom was the youngest, being only five. Of course, that's not counting little Jennie, but she was just a babe in arms. I was standing there trying to stop the wind blowing my hair our of place, and watching all those faces going past. I watched their eyes. Heenans, Thompsons, Ryans, Ryders. I watched Ryders real close. Quiglys, Tooheys, Glendennings, Madigans, Mahers . . . I never forgot any of those faces . . . ever. *(Pause)* It was before sun-up that mother left to go to Goderich that day. I was the only one that saw her go. There, in the grey half-light of a misty April morning, I watched her get into the buggy and head off towards Lucan, to catch the early coach to Goderich.

(Will watches her leave as if through a window. The others join him at the window and all watch. Then they settle down on one side of the stage to wait. The following dialogue echoes from all corners of the stage, distant and surreal.)

One: Words . . . .

Two: Rolling over the barren ground.

Three: Blown across the wasteland.

One: Words.

Four: Words in the wind.

Five: A handspike frozen cold.

Six: Pointing into the night.

Four: And nowhere to hide, nowhere to hide.

Seven: To be hanged by the neck.

Eight: By the neck until death.

Nine: Until death.

Johannah: Jim! Jim!

One: The lighting silhouettes the trees by the far field.

Two: The damp and the dreams.

Three: Soft folds in the blue sky.

Four: And blood on the clouds by the edge of the day.

Five: A bird sang, unseen.

Six: A long time to be running.

Seven: A long time.

Eight: A long time.

Nine: A long time.

(These words echo for a while, then fade as the music fades. The music indicates the passage of time, as the focus shifts to the boys who are waiting. This can be an improvised scene in mime. For example, they may see someone and rush to the window, only to find it isn't her. They relax. Build the tension of waiting. Finally, they see her coming. They all tense up and look at one another. There is the sound of a buggy pulling up. A silence. Then, Mrs. Donnelly enters.)

Johannah: It's a reprieve.

(A moment's silence, and then they all jump around whooping for joy. They fall silent as Jim Donnelly appears under guard and in chains. He says farewell to the children, and finally Johannah. He tries to put his arms around her, but finds he can't. He kisses her goodbye, then exits with his guard. There is the sound of a train pulling out of a station, and they all wave goodbye. They slowly move back and sit as if spending an evening at home. Mrs. Donnelly sews and the children read or play with games. Slide 24 — warm colour — red.)

Will Donnelly: So we began to wait. The sentence had been changed to seven years at Kingston Prison, and there wasn't much we could do but put on a brave face and sit it out. It was hard work, and we all began to grow up fast. We closed the ranks as we had done before, and learned that by being close we were safe. So, we kept ourselves to ourselves as much as we could. There was something growing around us — we knew it was there. It frightened us — always did — but we never showed it. The first of seven winters was coming up. We had to keep working.

(This is a mime and music scene to cover the seven years during which Jim Donnelly was away in prison. During the song, the company acts out various farming scenes.)

LUCAN

SCALE 500 FT AN INCH.

Drawn by Jno Rogers.

Farm Lot Nº 27 Con IV.

(Town map circa 1878)

Johannah *(sings)*:
> When the snows have dusted starlight
> On the autumn's faded leaves,
> And the winter winds are blowing half a gale,
> Those cold days just recall
> The coldest of them all
> The day they took my Jim to jail.
>
> One year going
> Kids are growing
> Winds are blowing cold
> Seeds for sowing
> Money owing
> And young men getting bold
> Arms are stronger
> Memories longer
> Yes, boys, you're growing old.

Patrick Donnelly *(ten years old)*: Father never meant to kill that man, did he?

Johannah: No, Patrick. It was done in the fury of a moment. But the law says someone's got to pay. *(She sings)*
> Three years going
> Kids are growing
> Yes, boys — you're growing old.

Boy 1: Hey, cripple!

Boy 2: It's wee Willy Donnelly and his gammy foot.

Boy 1: Where are you going, cripple? Looking for your father?

Boy 2: You'll not find him here.

Will Donnelly: You little bastards! I'll tan your hides.

Boy 1: You'll have to catch us first.

(He chases them. They dodge away.)

Boy 2: What's your father doing now? Killing men at Kingston prison?

(They scatter again. He catches one with the help of one of his brothers. William unclasps his belt and gives him a beating.)

Will Donnelly: This is a special present from the Donnellys. And when you go squealing to your folks, tell them that's what will happen to anyone who thinks we can't look after ourselves while our father's away.

(Several voices offstage sing the chorus while the dialogue goes on at the same time.)

Voices *(sing)*:
    Five years going
    Winds are blowing cold
    Seeds for sowing
    Money owing
    And young men getting bold
    Arms are stronger
    Memories longer
    Yes, boys, you're growing old.

Jennie: What does Papa look like?

Johannah: Well . . . he's a big, strong man with dark hair and . . . .

Jennie: Does he look like Will or Pat or John?

Johannah *(laughs)*: He looks a bit like all of them, to tell the truth.

Jennie: When's he coming home?

Johannah: Just two more years, pet.

Jennie: Two years is an awful long time.

Johannah: Aye . . . it's an awful long time. *(Fade up last lines of "Five Years Going" chorus. Will and his brother return to centre stage)* Boys, boys! You've been fighting again!

Will Donnelly: We had to, mother. They were saying bad things about Pa.

Johannah: They may be saying bad things about Pa, but they'll be saying worse things about us. I think I'm raising devils instead of sons. I wish to heaven your father was here.

Voices: Seven years going
Kids are growing
Yes, boys . . . you're growing old.

(There is the sound of a key in a lock and a prison door opening. Johannah and the kids react.)

Johannah: Seven years gone. Your father's coming home.

(Johannah lines the kids up and makes sure they're smart. Jim enters. He greets them all one by one and tries to guess their names. This can be an improvised scene.)

Jim Donnelly: Boys . . . ! I never believed you'd get so big in seven years. You've all worked hard . . . I'm proud of you.

Johannah: There's a lot of people glad you're back, Jim.

Jim Donnelly: Aye, and there's a lot who wish I wasn't. But, they'll think twice about tampering with me, now my boys are getting big. Just look at the size of them!

Will Donnelly: There's no one in Biddulph dares push us around. I never been beat yet.

John Donnelly: Just listen to him, will you? I'm as good a fighter as you any day.

Will Donnelly: Are you, hell!

Jim Donnelly: Boys . . . don't be fighting yourselves. There's plenty of people to fight without turning on your brothers.

Johannah: Come inside, Jim, and rest. You must be tired.

Jim Donnelly: Not yet, Johannah. I want to walk around my fields. Twenty-one years ago we stood here and looked out into the bush, and dreamed of a good life. For a long time, I'd forgotten what that felt like . . . now, I remember. Come with me.

(Jim and Johannah exit. Mulligan enters.)

Mulligan: Jim Donnelly was back. The year was 1866.

Will Donnelly: So, you reckon you can beat me, eh?

John Donnelly: I reckon so.

Will Donnelly: Well . . . you know what that means.

(They take off their coats and begin a lively scrap. The rest of the Donnelly boys cheer them on excitedly, as it is obviously a friendly fight. They freeze during Mulligan's speech.)

Mulligan: 1867, and James Donnelly pistol-whipped Constable Kennedy. *(Fight starts again)* 1869, and Tom Donnelly bit Constable Berryman's nose off in a fight. *(Fight starts again)* 1871, and Will buys a stagecoach line. The seven deadly sons, and Will was still the leader.

(Will gets John in a grip and John gives in. Will is congratulated by the others. Martin McLaughlin enters.)

Pat Donnelly: Hey . . . it's Martin McLaughlin!

Will Donnelly: Hello, Martin. How are you?

McLaughlin: Fine, Will. What the hell have you been doing?

Will Donnelly: Oh, just a friendly scrap with my brother. If you ever want a good fight, Martin, you know where to come.

McLaughlin: Fighting's not my line of business, Will.

Pat Donnelly *(sarcastically)*: His "line of business" is school work.

Will Donnelly: There's nothing wrong with that, Pat. You could do with a bit yourself.

James Donnelly *(mocking)*: We'll have to watch our words, boys. Our Will is a learned man. Remember that love letter he sent to Maggie Thompson? "Oh, me darling Maggie, I love your heavenly face, your angelic disposition . . . . "

John Donnelly: And your big tits.

Will Donnelly: You bastard! *(He chases John as the boys scream with laughter.)*

James Donnelly: Oh, it was written in such a beautiful scholarly hand.

Will Donnelly: Another crack from you and you'll feel my beautiful scholarly hand on your jaw. Clear off, you lot, me and Martin is in need of an intelligent discussion.

James Donnelly: Come on, boys, Let's go chase some of Grouchy Ryder's cows.

(They exit.)

Will Donnelly: Don't mind them, Martin, they're good lads when they want to be. *(He notices a worried look on McLaughlin's face)* What's up? You look troubled.

McLaughlin: Will . . . I came up because . . . well, I thought I'd better tell you something I heard in town. They're saying it was one of your boys that robbed the post office at Granton last week.

Will Donnelly: Is that right? Well, if one of my brothers stole that, the bastard's keeping it to himself.

McLaughlin: They're also laying the burning of Maher's barn at your door.

Will Donnelly: For chrissakes! None of us were in on that.

McLaughlin: I just thought I'd better warn you . . . they're laying a lot of things on you.

Will Donnelly: You don't believe them, do you, Martin?

McLaughlin: Believe them? Of course not.

Will Donnelly: It wasn't our boys, Martin, you must believe that.

McLaughlin: I do, Will. But the rest of the town isn't so sure.

Will Donnelly: To hell with the rest of the town! There's a lot of people been mighty jealous of me since I got my stage line.

McLaughlin: How's that going, Will?

Will Donnelly: Damned well! I'll have Flannagan's off the road in a year, no trouble. You're not doing too bad yourself. I hear you're going to be our next magistrate.

McLaughlin: Yes . . . chances are pretty good now.

Will Donnelly: That's what learning does for you. You'll be a good one too, Martin.

McLaughlin: I'm going to do my best for the people of Lucan.

Will Donnelly: I'm sure you will. Come on, let's drink to the people of Lucan. I've got a bottle of whisky needs finishing. I stole it out of old man Thompson's shed last Monday.

McLaughlin: You stole it! I heard he keeps a closer count of his whisky bottles than he does of his own children.

Will Donnelly: I know, but I got Maggie to help me.

McLaughlin: Maggie! You really are sweet on Maggie Thompson!

Will Donnelly: She's a fine girl.

McLaughlin: Oh boy . . . if old man Thompson finds out, there'll be trouble.

Will Donnelly: Nothing I can't handle. Come on. Let's drink to it.

(They exit. Slide 25 — inside a church. Three women enter, chattering to themselves, and sit down.)

Annie: Come on, girls . . . I promised Father Connolly we'd have a parcel ready for Ireland by Friday.

Janet: I've nearly finished this one.

(Janet is obviously very pregnant. She holds up a sweater. It is a very tatty piece of work with big holes in it.)

Agnes: Isn't that nice?

Annie: That'll help someone back home.

Agnes: We're not exactly sitting pretty ourselves. I mean, they've got a famine — and we've got the Donnellys. I'm not sure who's better off.

(Dora enters.)

Dora: I'm sorry I'm late, girls. My Henry got blind drunk at the McLeans again, and I had to drag him home.

Annie: Men . . . they're not worth the bother.

Agnes: That's easy enough said, but where would we be without them? I'd like to see you protect yourself against the Donnellys.

Dora: I'd like to see Henry protect me against the Donnellys.

Janet: I know . . . it's terrible, isn't it? All these goings on. My Albert says they're a wicked bunch.

Annie: He's right. They'd steal anything that wasn't nailed down.

Dora: That's a lot of nonsense. They're wild, but no worse than a dozen others.

Janet: Well, I don't know. I just leave it to Albert. But he says all them barn-burnings are being done by him and his sons.

Agnes: My father says the same. After all, it's got a lot worse since Jim Donnelly got back from prison. I think it would have been better if they'd hanged him, rather than letting a murderer back on the streets.

Dora: There's fights every Saturday night that could end in someone getting killed, just the same as the fight Farrell and Donnelly were in. It was a drunken brawl, not a murder. And wasn't it the Donnellys that looked after Farrell's young son ever since the killing?

Annie: That was the least they could do, I think. Don't you think so, Janet?

Janet: Oh, I don't know . . . I just leave it to Albert.

Dora: Well, I think that there's a lot of people in this town committing crimes, just because they know that the Donnellys will get the blame.

Janet: Well, I must admit they've always been very nice to me, but my boys say they throw their weight around a bit. They're all very strong, you know, and my Albert says . . . .

Agnes: That William is the worst of the bunch . . . that affair with Maggie Thompson. Fancy trying to take her by force.

Janet: Albert says they beat old Thompson up.

Dora: That's what Thompson said, but I saw him the morning after — and he didn't have a scratch on him!

Janet: Oh, I don't know anything about it. I just . . . .

Dora: Leave it to Albert.

Janet: Well, he knows about these things.

Dora *(sarcastically)*: Oh . . . I'm sure he does.

Agnes: Isn't it terrible . . . all we seem to talk about nowadays is them Donnellys.

Janet: Well, I must be going. *(She gets up.)*

Annie: Oh, by the way . . . when's the baby due?

Janet: August.

Agnes: How many's that?

Janet: Six. Four boys and a girl — so far.

Dora: Another mouth to feed!

Annie: Going to have any more?

Janet: I'm not sure right now.

Dora: I'm sure you will. Just leave it to Albert.

(Tim Mulligan staggers in singing.)

Mulligan:
>There once was a plumber called Lee,
>Who was plumbing his girl by the sea.
>Said the girl, "Stop your plumbing
>There's someone coming!"
>Said the plumber, still plumbing, "It's me!"

(He roars with laughter. The ladies are shocked. He sees them) Oh, begging your pardon, ladies.

Agnes: I think we'd better be going.

(They begin to exit.)

Mulligan: Just a minute, ladies. *(He gets his pipe out)* Do you have a match?

Dora: Yes . . . your face and a horse's arse.

(Slide 26 — dark colour — blue.)

Mulligan: Jasus . . . she's a sharp one. *(All the ladies exit. Mulligan staggers around for a moment, and then as an afterthought says —)* Would you be after a kiss then? *(He sits down and takes a swig from a bottle)* It was the very worst time in Lucan. The very worst. There was fires and robbings like you wouldn't believe. It was a time when decent folks lived in fear of night, because you never knew what was waiting for you in the shadows.

(Lighting effects of flames in distance. Sound — the clamour of an alarm bell. Mr. Toohey enters with a woman and an old man, as if helping them out of a burning house. He rushes towards the fire again, but the constable stops him.)

Toohey: Christ! Just look at it. The whole house gone. The whole damn thing! Those bastards!

Constable: I'm afraid we'll not save it, Mr. Toohey.

Toohey: Of course you won't. Those bastards know how to set a good fire.

Constable: Have you any idea who may have done this?

Toohey: Have I an idea . . . ? Christ! I know who set the damned fire. Those bloody Donnellys.

(McLaughlin enters.)

McLaughlin: I got here as soon as I heard, Constable. Is there any chance of saving it?

Constable: I'm afraid not, sir.

McLaughlin: I'm sorry about this, Mr. Toohey.

Toohey: You're sorry, are you? Well, that's great, but it's no bloody good to me! Call yourselves the law! What the hell's the use of the law in this godforsaken town?

Constable: He believes it was the Donnellys, Mr. McLaughlin.

Toohey: My barns went two months ago, and now my farmhouse. You don't need to tell me who did it. I sold two of my best thoroughbreds to Flannagan's stage line last week. That bastard Will Donnelly wanted them, but I told him I'd never sell good horses to a Blackfoot. There you see the result.

All *(sing)*:
>Burn, burn,
>Cut and burn,
>The night is long
>When it's your turn.
>
>They cleared the land with axe and fire,
>They made the earth their home.
>Their flames became a funeral pyre,
>The seeds of death were sown.

Flannagan: My name's Flannagan — I own the stage line. I was driving down to London last week when the Donnelly coach comes up behind me . . . driving hard . . . shouting for room to pass. Well, I whipped up the horses so we're both going at a pace, and that damn fool Will tries to pass . . . to knock me off the road. I held my ground . . . and Will's screaming and hollering . . . but God must'a been watching, 'cos it's him that goes flying into the ditch . . . and he knows he's beat fair and square. *(Pause)* Yesterday, I awoke and found all the tongues cut out of my horses, and my coach chopped to firewood. I had to shoot all my horses . . . they were screaming in agony. Have you ever heard a horse scream? It's not a pretty sound . . . the blood was gushing out of their mouths. I'd only bought the horses a few days before from Mr. Toohey. That's the kind of people those Donnellys are.

All *(sing)*:
>Burn, burn,
>Cut and burn,
>The night is long
>When it's your turn.
>
>The night is dark, the clouds are deep,
>A twig snaps in the breeze.
>A farmer jumps, throws off his sleep
>And curses those Black Donnellys.

Pat Donnelly *(goes to Will)*: Will . ... I just come from Andy Keefe's. A couple of Ryder's boys took him for a walk in a barrel of thorns . . . and on our account, too.

Will Donnelly: That's a damned Whiteboy trick . . . but why on our account, Pat?

Pat Donnelly: They was saying we burned Toohey's barn, and he says he was at our place that night and none of us was out . . . and they says he's a liar and was probably in on it, too . . . and dragged him out and . . . .

Will Donnelly: Boys . . . this account needs settling. If the Devil likes to dance in flames, then the Ryders will feel well at home tonight.

John Donnelly: Will . . . is there no other way?

Will Donnelly: Those Ryder boys could club their grandmother to death in the constable's office, and we'd get blamed for it. Let's give them something real to complain about.

All *(sing)*:
>Burn, burn,
>Cut and burn,
>The night is long
>When it's your turn.

No one sleeps in Lucan town
No one sleeps
No one sleeps
No one sleeps in Lucan town.

Thompson: I want to see some action against them Donnellys. That young pup Will Donnelly came to my house to try and steal my daughter away, after I'd told him I'd be seen dead before I'd have a Donnelly in the family. He came with his brothers, threatened me with a gun and beat me up.

Man 1: My cows got poisoned.

Man 2: My barns burned.

Man 3: I was beaten up and robbed.

Man 4: The London Free Press 1877 . . . matters have now reached such a crisis in Lucan that nobody thinks of going out at night without a revolver, and a person who goes on another person's property after dark goes at the risk of his life. For, if the owner happens to be a nervous man, he may shoot first, and make inquiries afterwards.

(Father Connolly enters.)

Woman 1: Help us.

Woman 2: Help us, Father Connolly.

Woman 3: There are bad people in this town, Father Connolly.

Woman 1: They are Catholic, Father . . . .

Woman 3: But their friends are Protestants and Orangemen.

Father Connolly: I cannot condemn a man for how he chooses his friends.

Man 1: But worse . . . they kill and burn.

Man 2: And burn and steal . . . .

Man 3: And steal and kill.

Man 4: We live in terror. They are devils, Father.

Man 5: They are the scourge of the township.

Man 6: Rotten to the core.

Man 7: They cut out the tongues of Watson's horses.

Man 8: And when they wouldn't die . . . .

Man 9: Slit their throats.

Father Connolly: But what proof do you have?

Woman 1: I was told.

Woman 2: I was told.

Woman 3: Here in Biddulph, we know these things.

Father Connolly: But the law, what of the law?

Woman 3: Biddulph is beyond the law.

Woman 1: Speak against them, and your horses are killed.

Woman 2: Your homes are burned.

Woman 3: Biddulph is beyond the law.

(Martin McLaughlin moves to Father Connolly.)

McLaughlin: Father Connolly, we need your help. We must form a vigilante committee.

(The stage grows very dark and there is the sound of thunder. After the thunder, the slow and mournful tolling of a bell.)

Johannah: That's the saddest sound I ever heard, Jim. It's giving me a terrible fear, deep to my stomach.

Jim Donnelly: Johannah, our eldest son is dead.

Johannah: How did he die?

Man 1: James Donnelly was shot while trying to fire the McLean's Hotel.

Man 2: A bullet in the groin.

Woman 1: Lead poisoning.

Woman 2: Gunshot wounds.

Man 3: He was knifed in a fight.

Woman 3: Shot by a fire-watcher.

Man 1: A pistol ball in the stomach.

Jim Donnelly: The doctor said it was appendicitis.

Men *(1, 2, 3)*: One down,

Women *(1, 2, 3)*: And six to go.

(Everyone kneels.)

All: Our Father, who art in heaven, give us this day our daily bread, and forgive us our trespasses, except that they be Donnellys.

McLaughlin: Father Connolly, we must form a vigilante committee.

Father Connolly: From what I have seen, I think you are right. We must band together to protect ourselves and maintain peace. It is my duty to keep the peace within my flock. We must find out who are the perpetrators of these crimes.

McLaughlin: The Donnellys, Father. You need look no further.

Father Connolly: You seem very certain.

All: We are, Father.

(The company forms a large circle on the set with Father Connolly in centre stage.)

All *(sing)*:
>We're only honest farmers,
>And we've no mind to kill.
>But if our homes are threatened,
>Then, by Christ, we will.
>
>Of all the thieves in Canada
>This family's the worst.
>Before they come to murder us
>We'll go and kill them first.
>
>And mothers tell their children
>To bolt their windows tight,
>For the Devil and the Donnellys
>Are riding past tonight.

McLaughlin: We need a leader. Someone who does not fear the Donnellys. I believe we have a man. I also have reason to believe that he will be the next constable of Lucan.

All:
>You may condemn our actions
>And say they caused much pain.
>But if you'd lived in Lucan town
>You would have done the same.

(James Carroll enters from upstage, and slowly moves towards Connolly. He is a big roughneck, dressed in common labourer's clothes.)

>And so the men of Lucan town
>Knew well what must be done.
>We'll stand and fight the Donnellys
>We'll make the bastards run.
>
>We found a fierce leader
>Who all would come to hear
>They called him . . . .

James Carroll *(extending his hand to Connolly)*: James Carroll. I'll drive them out of Lucan . . . or see them buried here.

(Curtain.)

(Canadian stage coach ticket circa 1880's)

Act two Tableau as the end of Act one. Also onstage are Jim, Johannah and Will Donnelly.

Father Connolly: An oath must be taken. *(He goes to each man and woman onstage with a book which they sign. He is accompanied by Carroll. As Connolly reads out each section of the oath, the company repeats it)* We the undersigned —

All: We the undersigned,

Father Connolly: Roman Catholics

All: Roman Catholics

Father Connolly: Of Saint Patrick's

All: Of Saint Patrick's

Father Connolly: Of Biddulph

All: Of Biddulph

Father Connolly: Solemnly pledge ourselves

All: Solemnly pledge ourselves

(They reach Jim Feeheeley. He hesitates.)

Carroll: Jim Feeheeley. Why will you not sign?

Feeheeley: Tom's my best friend. I will not swear against him.

(Carroll grabs Feeheeley in an arm hold. Father Connolly goes on with the book. He pretends not to see what Carroll is doing.)

Father Connolly: Pledge ourselves to aid

All: Pledge ourselves to aid

Father Connolly: Our spiritual director

All: Our spiritual director

Father Connolly: And parish priest

All: And parish priest

Feeheeley: Aaagh! You'll break my arm, Carroll!

Carroll: You'll help the committee when the time comes.

Father Connolly: In the discovery and putting down

All: In the discovery and putting down

Father Connolly: Of crime in this mission.

All: Of crime in this mission.

Feeheeley: I'll do as you say, Carroll.

Father Connolly: So help me God.

All: So help me God.

Will Donnelly: They've got up some kind of committee, and there's talk of an oath.

Jim Donnelly: Aye . . . and they've made that bully-boy Carroll the constable. There's method in all this.

Carroll: Why haven't you signed the oath, Mulligan?

Mulligan: Oh . . . well, I can't read, so I don't know what it's about.

Carroll: I'll read it to you.

Mulligan: Oh . . . oh. I can feel one of my deaf spells coming on.

McLaughlin: Let him be, Carroll. He's not important.

(During the signing, some people sign and some don't. Carroll takes careful note of each. This divides the group up into Carroll's cronies and the rest. At the end of the scene, those who signed gather around Carroll, and the rest exit.)

All: We solemnly pledge ourselves to aid our parish priest in the putting down of crimes committed by — *(overlap — "the rest")* unknown parti — unknown parties — unknown parties — *("Carroll's cronies")* the Don nellys — the Donnellys —

Johannah: Why must we stay in Biddulph? Why must we stay in a town that hates us?

Jim Donnelly: There's thirty years work in this land. We can't pack up and start again. All this will pass.

(Jim and Johannah exit. Carroll and his cronies lounge about in the background, like a gang looking for trouble. Mulligan moves downstage.)

Mulligan: Committees, oaths and God knows what else! I might as well have stayed in Tipperary. Myself . . . I'm staying well out of this. I have a feeling this deaf spell is going to last quite a while. There's too many strange things going on for my liking. *(He notices the gang and decides that it's time to exit. Carroll blocks his way)* Ah . . . evening there, constable. Lovely night for a walk. *(Pause)* Waiting for someone, are you?

Carroll: That's right . . . for a friend of the committee.

Mulligan: Well . . . I'll leave you to it.

Carroll: You're a friend of the committee, aren't you, Mulligan?

Mulligan: Me? Why, sure . . . you know me . . . everybody's friend.

Carroll: Everybody's?

Mulligan: Well, not everybody. Look, I have to be going . . . pubs are open. 'Bye!

Carroll: There was a party at the Donnellys' Saturday last. I was wondering if you were there.

Mulligan: Sure, if I can remember where the hell a party was, it wasn't worth going to.

Carroll: Have you been hobnobbing with the Donnellys?

Mulligan: I've always said, Carroll, I'd rather die than be buried near a Donnelly.

Carroll: Just give me a straight answer . . . were you at that party?

Mulligan: I swear by the holy bones of King Billy's horse I don't remember a thing.

(Carroll sees a bottle in Mulligan's pocket and takes it out.)

Carroll: Where did you get this from? Looks expensive.

Mulligan: Ah, no, no . . . that's turpentine. For cleaning me boots.

Carroll: Smells like whisky.

Mulligan: It's rot-gut. The very worst . . . my word of honour.

Carroll: Smells pretty good to me. *(Swigs it)* Mmmm! What do you think, Pat? *(Hands it to Quigly.)*

Mulligan: It burns holes in iron, I tell you.

Quigly *(drinks)*: That's good stuff. The kind the Donnellys would drink.

(Hogan grabs it.)

Hogan: I'll tell you if it's good whisky. *(He takes a large swig.)*

Mulligan: Sure it's whisky, but it's mixed with castor oil.

(Hogan stops abruptly and spits it out.)

Hogan: What?

Mulligan: Well, it tastes rotten, but it gives you a better run for your money. *(Someone else grabs the bottle, drinks, and passes it along to Carroll. Mulligan goes after it)* Take me life if you must, but I need me whisky!

(Carroll suddenly grabs Mulligan viciously.)

Carroll: Alright, you dirty little scum! Think you're clever with your smart-ass jokes, and your bad memory. You were at the Donnellys' Saturday night, and if you don't tell us who was there, we'll cut your nose right down the middle. *(He gets out a knife.)*

Mulligan: Don't cut me, Carroll. I don't know nuthin'!

Carroll: Names, Mulligan . . . names!

Mulligan: In the name of heaven! I was blind drunk.

Carroll: You're a lying pig. *(He is about to cut him.)*

Mulligan: I don't know nuthin' . . . I don't know nuthin' . . . ask him *(pointing at Hogan)* . . . he was there!

(Carroll puts Mulligan down. Mulligan rushes out terrified, the others look at Hogan.)

Hogan: Come on, now. You wouldn't believe an old drunk like him. *(Silence)* Wasn't it me that beat up John Donnelly at that donnybrook down at the Queen's?

Quigly: You never did, Hogan.

Hogan: I did so . . . you ask anyone who was there.

Purtell: I've heard Pat Donnelly's a friend of yours.

Hogan: That's a damned lie. I hate Pat Donnelly . . . I hate all the Donnellys . . . *(sensing that they don't believe him)* I hate them . . . Carroll . . . I hate them!

(Carroll makes a sign to Madigan and a couple of others, and they exit.)

Carroll: That's alright, Hogan — I believe you . . . we all believe you . . . right, lads?

((The others agree, and Madigan enters.)

Madigan: Hey, look what we found.

(They bring on a barrel.)

Carroll: Now, that's a fine barrel . . . but, as constable, I must say it looks uncommon like the barrel we just passed in McCullough's front yard.

Madigan: Sure looks the same, don't it? But this one just fell off a wagon.

Carroll: Well, I know you're an honest man, Mike, so I'll take your word. Anyway, McCullough's a Protestant, so he ain't covered by the law . . . and we need it more than him.

Hogan: Hey . . . we going to do the barrel of thorns trick? We going to find ourselves a Donnelly?

Carroll: Something like that. Come on, boys, let's fill her up. *(They all grab thorns and branches and put them in the barrel)* Looks pretty good. Like to see a Donnelly in there, eh, Hogan?

Hogan: Sure would, Carroll . . . that's where they belong.

Carroll: And all the Blackfeet should be in there, too, right?

Hogan: Right.

Carroll: And all the friends of Donnellys?

Hogan: Right.

Carroll: And all the people who sneak off and neighbour with Donnellys behind our backs?

(Hogan is beginning to realize something strange is going on and begins to get nervous.)

Hogan *(pause)*: Right.

Carroll: Now, I'm a bit worried about this barrel. I don't think it's big enough for a Donnelly or a Donnelly-lover. Would you mind getting in it to check it out?

Hogan *(frightened)*: It looks big enough to me, Carroll.

Carroll: Well, I really need someone in it to judge properly. Just for a moment, now.

(The others grab him and put him in the barrel.)

Hogan: Please . . . please . . . .

Carroll: Now, don't be getting so upset, Hogan. Like I said, this barrel can only hurt Donnellys or Donnelly-lovers. I know some people have been saying you're neighbouring with the Donnellys . . .

Hogan: No, Carroll . . . not me . . . I promise . . . .

Carroll: So, we'll just roll you around a bit, and if the thorns hurt you, then we'll know you've been neighbouring with the Donnellys. If they don't, then we know that God and the Pope are watching over you.

Hogan: Nooooooo!

(They begin to roll him around in the barrel, and Hogan screams in pain. The others enjoy this and shout with delight. They lay the barrel on its side and Hogan tries to crawl out. Carroll stands on Hogan's hand.)

Carroll: This town, Hogan, is very much like that barrel of thorns you were just in. It ain't comfortable to live in no more. And we both know who the thorns are, don't we? And when you cut thorns, you use a sharp knife. Stay away from them, Hogan, or you'll get cut too . . . understand me? *(Hogan nods)* Now run along.

(He runs off to the jeers of the gang. A spot comes up on McLaughlin.

McLaughlin: Carroll! *(Carroll draws his hat in mock reverence)* For the last time, Carroll. Do you have to use such crude methods?

Carroll: You should join in the fun sometime.

(A spot comes up on Father Connolly.)

Father Connolly: Carroll, I don't approve of the way you're handling this.

Carroll: Christ!

Father Connolly: When we made you constable . . . .

Carroll: You made me constable to put down the Donnellys. I've got Pat, John and Will Donnelly up for assault, and Tom for arson, and I sure as hell didn't get them from pussy-footing around like McLaughlin.

Father Connolly: I cannot approve of your methods. You must remember that we are doing this for the good of the people. We must not usurp the authority given to us by God. Our object is to eliminate fear — not create it.

Carroll *(mocking)*: Yes, Father, I shall remember that.

Father Connolly: Remember, my son.

(The spot fades on Father Connolly.)

Carroll: Goddamned priest!

McLaughlin: Carroll . . . have you got hold of James Keefe yet?

Carroll: No, he's next.

McLaughlin: I also want you to get your hands on Will Farrell, but I warn you, he'll be tough.

Carroll: Farrell. That name's familiar. Didn't the old man murder a Farrell, and then get a reprieve?

McLaughlin: Yes . . . this Will Farrell's his son. The Donnellys looked after him ever since the murder, and now he's as bad as they are.

Carroll: They looked after him, eh? I confess I'm surprised. I wouldn't have thought they'd have it in them.

McLaughlin: Never mind that. We've got business to do. There's a good chance of arresting some of the Donnelly brothers tonight. I've got the warrants here.

Carroll: The case is strong enough?

McLaughlin: It's strong enough.

Carroll: Where will I find them?

McLaughlin: There's a wedding today, and the reception will be at Fitzhenry's Hotel this evening. They'll be there.

(Slide 27 — Fitzhenry's Hotel. The scene becomes a wedding reception in its later and more rowdy stages. There is much noise and singing. John and Will Donnelly are there with Will Farrell. A very drunk man with a pint mug of beer in his hand climbs on a table or level.)

Man *(drunk — sings)*:
>Let's drink to he
>Who is no more free
>No more free
>No more free.

(Everyone joins in.)

All *(sing)*:
>Let's drink to he
>Who is no more free
>No more free-i-oh . . .

(At the last line, they all take a swig from their glasses. The drunk takes his beer, and while someone lies down on the ground, he pours it down the second man's throat from on top of the table. The drunk sings as he does this.)

Man *(drunk — sings)*:
>Open your gob
>And let liquor run in
>Liquor run in
>Liquor run in.

(Everyone joins in.)

All *(sing)*:
>Open your gob
>And let liquor run in
>Liquor run in-i-oh . . .

(Everyone takes another swig as Carroll and two deputies enter. Carroll fires a shot in the air. Everyone freezes.)

Jim Donnelly: What's up, Carroll?

Carroll: I have warrants for the arrest of John Donnelly, William Donnelly and William Farrell.

Jim Donnelly: Ah, come on, Carroll. It's a party . . . have a few drinks first.

(Carroll pushes him out of the way. He looks at Will Donnelly.)

Carroll: Let's go, Donnelly.

Will Donnelly: So you managed to buy yourself some more witnesses, Carroll?

Carroll: You three! Move!

Will Donnelly: If you want us, Carroll, you know what to do.

(Carroll is covered by his deputies, and moves warily towards Will Donnelly with handcuffs. Will holds his hands out for him. Just as he is about to put them on, Will hits him. A struggle ensues, but the deputies cannot shoot for fear of hitting Carroll. Will Farrell pulls out a gun and shoots a deputy in the stomach. Farrell runs for it. But the Donnellys are taken off their guard by the shot and are caught. The stage clears as people chase Farrell and take off the Donnellys, leaving Carroll. A spot comes up on Father Connolly. Slide 28 — Courthouse.)

Carroll: We've got them, Father Connolly! We took them at Fitzhenry's Hotel.

(A judge enters.)

Judge: Before I pass sentence, I would like to say a few words regarding this case against the Donnellys. From the evidence, it seems that they have been infected with the spirit that is the bane of the neighbourhood of Lucan. Now, I have no doubt they can be generous, warmhearted, and would make good friends. But, there is no doubt they make bad enemies. At the same time, I must say to the prosecution that the number of times you have dragged this family into court with just a modicum of evidence is a gross waste of the court's time. For resisting arrest, I sentence you to six months hard labour. Take them away.

(The judge exits.)

Carroll: Damnation! Minimum bloody sentence!

Father Connolly: It is disappointing, but we must have faith in the will of God. In his will is our peace.

Carroll: "Peace" . . . for six months, and what then? Back where we bloody well began. Look, Connolly, you know damned well . . . .

Father Connolly: No! We must keep within the law.

Carroll: The law! What the hell's the good of a law that doesn't know a murderer or a thief when it sees one? We risk our goddamned lives bringing the bastards in, and all the law does is give them a few months inside and a pat on the arse. You'll be screaming for the law when they come to murder you in your bed one night, and a fat lot of good it'll do you.

Father Connolly: I'll not consent to it!

Carroll: I've got over forty vigilantes waiting, and they'll not wait forever.

Father Connolly: We must learn to wait.

(Around them in the shadows there are people. A single spot picks out the judge.)

Judge: The Queen versus Thomas Donnelly.

Man 1: Arson.

Judge: The Queen versus William Donnelly, John Donnelly, William Farrell, James Keefe, William Denby.

Men *(1, 2)*: Assault.

Judge: The Queen versus William Farrell.

Men *(1, 2, 3)*: Shooting with intent to kill.

Judge: The Queen versus William and John Donnelly.

Men *(1, 2, 3, 4)*: Assault.

Judge: The Queen versus James Donnelly.

Men *(1, 2, 3, 4, 5)*: Shooting with intent to kill.

Judge: John Donnelly.

Men *(1, 2, 3, 4, 5, 6)*: Assault.

Judge: Thomas and James Donnelly.

Men *(1, 2, 3, 4, 5, 6, 7)*: Arson.

Judge: Thomas Donnelly.

Men *(1, 2, 3, 4, 5, 6, 7, 8)*: Larceny.

Judge: James and William Donnelly.

Men *(1, 2, 3, 4, 5, 6, 7, 8, 9)*: Assault.

Judge: James and Patrick Donnelly.

Men *(1, 2, 3, 4, 5, 6, 7, 8, 9, 10)*: Assault.

Father Connolly: We must learn to wait.

(Jim and Johannah enter as the others recede. Slide 29 — cold colour blue.)

Jim Donnelly: It's a sad day when a father sees his sons dragged into the courts like this.

Johannah: The charges are rigged, Jim. You know that.

Jim Donnelly: It doesn't make it a hell of a lot easier. Why are they using us like this?

Johannah: They won't rest until we leave.

(Pause.)

Jim Donnelly: I know, Johannah. I guess we've both known it for a long time. I'm too tired, Johannah. I'm getting old, and I'm too tired to fight, and too tired to run. *(Pause)* I've got a feeling deep in the pit of my stomach. It's like there's a rat gnawing at my innards. They're in my dreams as well. I find myself looking into the darkness, and all around there's these eyes watching me. Everywhere . . . everywhere I look. Hundreds of fat black rats . . . whispering and chattering and staring. Eyes full of hatred, and teeth dripping with disease. You can feel their hatred like hot spit burning your face. And all the little bastards are waiting. Waiting for the right time.

Johannah: It's only a dream, Jim.

Jim Donnelly: No, Johannah . . . I get the same feeling when I walk into town. I look into people's eyes and see the same thing, Johannah . . . I see the same goddamned thing!

(The stage is still surrounded by people in the shadows. They whisper without moving.)

All: Waiting
   'Til the time is right,
   Waiting
   Shadows in the night,
   Waiting.

Jim Donnelly: Christ! You think I can't feel it? You think I don't know what you're all thinking?

Johannah: Calm down, Jim . . . I never seen you so shaken up.

Jim Donnelly: Can't you see it? One by one they've stopped talking to us. One by one they've stopped coming around.

Johannah: You're just imagining things, Jim. We've still got a few good friends left.

Jim Donnelly: But how much longer, Johannah? How much longer until they're all gone?

All: Watching
   'Til the time is right,
   Watching
   Shadows in the night,
   Watching.

Jim Donnelly: They'd like to break us. They'd like to see us grovel. But we won't . . . we won't.

All: Waiting
   'Til the time is right,
   Waiting
   Shadows in the night,
   Waiting.

(Company exits. Jim moves to a table where he writes a letter in a slow and painful hand.)

Jim Donnelly: January 12th, 1880. Mr. Meredith: Sir — On the 15th of last month, Pat Ryder's barns were burned. All the vigilante committee at once pointed to my family as the ones that done it. Ryder found out that all my boys were at a wedding that night. He at once arrested me and my wife on suspicion. The trial has been postponed four different times, and although we are ready for trial at any time, they examined a lot of witnesses but can't find anything against us. Ryder swore that we lived neighbours to each other for thirty years and never had any difference, and had no reason for arresting us, only that we are blamed for everything. They are using us worse than mad dogs. They had the first trial in Lucan, and then adjourned to Granton simply to advertise us. I want you to handle the case on our behalf, and if there is any chance for damages, I want you to attack them at once, as they will never let us alone until some of them are made an example of. There is not the slightest cause for our arrest, and it seems hard to see a man and a woman over sixty years of age dragged around as laughing stocks. Yours truly, James Donnelly, Sr.

(Jim exits. Slide 30 — a small lighted window at night. It is the schoolroom where the vigilantes meet. The door creaks open, and a man enters with a limp. He talks in whispers with another man.)

Madigan: Looks like we're early.

Toohey *(entering)*: Brrrr . . . it's cold.

Madigan: He did say eight-thirty?

Toohey: Yeah. *(Pause)* Hey, what are we whispering for?

Madigan: I dunno. Hey . . . you got any whisky left?

(Toohey hands him a jar of whisky and they both drink. John Purtell enters. He is a large and rather stupid individual.)

Purtell: Hello, boys.

Madigan: Hello, John.

Purtell: You got a jar, eh?

VILLAGE OF LUCAN.

NAME.	LOCATION.	Date of Settlement.	NATIVITY.	POST OFFICE.	BUSINESS.
Armitage, J. R.	Main St.	1849	Canada	Lucan.	Merchant.
Atkinson, T. T.		1873	do	do	Carpenter.
Cann, L.	do	1861	do	do	Books & Stationery.
Cain, John F.	do	1869	do	do	Proprietor "Royal Hotel."
Farrell, John	do	1829	do	do	Druggist.
Gibson, S.	William St.	1867	do	do	Proprietor Planing Mills.
Gear, George	Main St.	1872	England	do	House Decorator.
Hutchins, W. H.	do	1863	Canada	do	Merchant & Reeve.
Hogg & Piefer		1876		do	Mfrs of Flax.
Haskett, W.	Market St.	1859	do	do	Farmer and Mill Owner.
Hersey, S. C.	Princess St.	1862	do	do	Grain Merchant.
Lotz, Rev. H. B.	Pastoral Residence.	1876	U. States	do	Roman Catholic Priest.
MacDiarmid, W.	William St.	1872	Canada	do	Barrister.
McLean, R.	Main St.	1844	Ireland	Lucan	Proprietor Central Hotel.
	do			"	" Queen's Hotel.
McFalls, R.	do	1854	Canada	do	Merchant
McCosh, J. D.	do	1861	do	do	Watchmaker & Jeweler.
Matheson, William.	do	1870	Scotland	do	Carpenter & Joiner.
McBride, William.		1873	Canada	do	Groceries, Flour, Feed, &c.
Orme, J. W.	do	1855	do	do	Butchers & Drovers.
Reid & Chisholm.				do	Livery & Pat. Spring Mfrs.
Shoebottom Bros.	William St.	1843	Scotland	do	Manager Bank of Commerce.
Thomas, J. E.	Main St.	1876	U. States	do	Job Printer.
Tom, James K.	William St.	1875	Canada	do	Prop. Walker House & Stage Line.
Walker, William.	do	1863	do	do	Tinsmith & Stoves.
Watts, J. C.	Main St.	1868	England	do	

(Prominent citizens of the community circa 1878)

Madigan: Want some?

Purtell: Sure. *(Takes a swig)* Hey . . . you know who I saw in town today? I saw Will Donnelly in town, and I says to him . . . I said, "Hey, there goes Will Donnelly!" An' I laughed at him, an' all my friends laughed at him. How 'bout that, eh?

Toohey: What did he say to that?

Purtell: He said, "Christ, is you's ever imbecilic." Whassat mean, eh?

Toohey: It means you're stupid.

Purtell: Oh.

(William Casey enters. He is a gentleman farmer.)

Casey: Good evening, Jim, Mike, and, er . . . .

Madigan: John.

Casey: Yes . . . John Purtell, of course. Well, how are you all? Damne cold, eh? He always chooses the coldest nights for his meetings.

Toohey: You reckon it'll be about Ryder's barn?

Casey: Without a doubt.

Madigan: You were a magistrate, Will. What do you think?

Casey: It'll never stick, I'm afraid.

Purtell: You mean he said I was stupid?

(Grouchy Ryder and Ed Ryan enter. They are both drunk.)

Ryder: *(sings to the tune of "Wild Colonial Boy")*:
    I am a wild colonial boy
    And Grouchy is my name,
    I was born and reared in Ireland
    At a place called Castlemaine.
Greetings to you all, boys . . . I smell blood in the air tonight.

Casey: Aye . . . and I smell whisky. Can you never stay sober, Ryder? It's an important meeting.

Ryder: Ah, magistrate . . . *(bows mockingly)* . . . no . . . ex-magistrate. Come to see that justice is done. Or perhaps your pockets are a-jingle with Donnelly silver.

(Suddenly tempers flare . . . they almost go for each other, but the others stop them.)

Toohey: Hold it, Grouchy. Take it easy! You boys been drinking?

Ryder: Sure we've been drinking, and do you want to know why we've been drinking? Tell him, Ed.

Ryan: You all know Grouchy's Sal, don't you?

Toohey: Sure, she's a fine mare.

Ryder: She's dead, boys. And I thought the Donnellys burning down my barn last week was bad enough. You know, I saw them do it. I saw them with my own eyes. And the court asks for evidence. Evidence! Christ . . . I saw them!

Ryan: And now they killed Sal. She broke her leg in a hole in the field over by the tracks.

Ryder: There was never a hole there before. I worked that field for thirty years, and there was never a hole there. Those bastard Donnellys put it there. And now they killed my best mare.

Purtell: You mean he said I was stupid?

Ryder: What are you talking about?

Toohey: Don't mind him, Grouchy.

Ryder: They're going to pay. Those bastards are going to pay, by Christ. They'll pay for burning my barn and killing my Sal. I'll make them pay for everything!

Casey: Not in the law courts they won't, Mr. Ryder.

Ryder: You bastard lawyers with all your "education". What the hell

Dudley Witney

do you know about justice? Pieces of paper and fancy words, that's all.

Toohey: Now cut it out, Grouchy! Will Casey is a friend of the committee. He wants to help us.

(Pat Quigly and several others enter.)

Ryder: Welcome, Pat, and all the rest of you. Welcome to our monthly parlour game. *(He laughs)* That's all this is, you know.

Quigly: Aye . . . I'm inclined to agree with you about that.

Ryder: You're a good man, Pat. Hey . . . let me tell you how it is. Now farmers like us . . . we're trained to use a pick and an axe . . . and once you've learned, you never forget. A constable . . . he's trained to use a gun and a club . . . and once he's learned, he never forgets. It's the same with your magistrates like McLaughlin and Casey here. They're trained to use the law and fancy words — and once they've learned, they never forget . . . right, Will? *(During this speech McLaughlin has entered)* And that's all we're going to get tonight, same as every other time.

McLaughlin: Thanks for the introduction, Grouchy.

Ryder: Oh, Christ.

Quigly: There's more'n a grain of truth in what he says, McLaughlin.

McLaughlin: Why weren't you at the trial this afternoon, Ryder?

Ryder: I was too drunk, damn you.

McLaughlin: For God's sake . . . it was your brother's barn that was burned. We could have used your evidence.

Madigan: How did it go, McLaughlin?

McLaughlin *(avoiding the question)*: Where's Carroll? He's late.

Toohey: I ain't seen him awhile, Mr. McLaughlin.

McLaughlin: Shall we start without him? *(General assent)* Very well. I have just come from the law courts. The case against the Donnellys for the burning of Mr. Ryder's barn is on the verge of falling through.

(Angry shouts from the crowd) Order . . . order, please! I admit that our efforts are continually being frustrated, but the process of the law requires evidence which no one is prepared to give. But, how do you expect people to come forward, if even you — the members of the committee — refuse to go to the trial?

Ryan: What's the point . . . they'd get off anyway.

McLaughlin: If we get the evidence, the law will put them away . . . I guarantee it!

Quigly: Sure, we'll give evidence . . . and get burned out for our troubles.

McLaughlin: I know it's difficult, but the law does work . . . we just got John Donnelly six months . . . .

Ryder: Six months! That means he'll be back with us before you can say barn-burning twice.

McLaughlin: We are doing our best to put the Donnellys behind bars, but while the law . . . .

Ryan: Bugger the law!

(Shouting and assent from crowd.)

McLaughlin: Please . . . let's have some order in here.

(Carroll enters. The crowd falls silent.)

Ryan: Hey . . . it's big, bad Carroll! The man who'd run the Donnellys out of town. You're doing a great bloody job, ain't you?

Carroll: Keep your mouth shut. *(He walks around the room looking at the men)* I suppose our lawyer here has told you about what happened at the law courts today.

McLaughlin: It can't be helped, Carroll. There's just not enough evidence.

Carroll: And how much longer do you intend to go on messing around with the law?

McLaughlin: Look, Carroll . . . the next time . . . .

Carroll: No! No more "next times", McLaughlin!

(Suddenly McLaughlin realizes what Carroll is thinking.)

McLaughlin: I know perfectly well what you want and I absolutely refuse. It would be stupid and dangerous.

Carroll: Well, I reckon that's up to the committee to decide. *(General assent)* Call the vote, McLaughlin.

(Shouts of assent from the crowd.)

McLaughlin: You're crazy! For God's sake . . . do you know what you're asking?

Carroll: Just call the vote.

McLaughlin: We can't vote on that. If Father Connolly . . . .

(Shouts from the crowd.)

Ryder: To hell with Father Connolly! Christ . . . you'd think the sun shines out of Father Connolly's arse. Father Connolly ain't got barns and livestock to lose.

Carroll: That's right, McLaughlin. People like you and Father Connolly can afford to wait. You're not farmers like the rest of the committee. You ain't going to wake up one morning and find a full year's harvest in ashes. You've never lost a thing at their hands.

Madigan: That's true, McLaughlin . . . they've never touched you.

Purtell: And Will Donnelly said I was stupid.

Toohey: Shut up, Purtell.

Carroll: You ain't got nothing to lose, McLaughlin, so you don't mind waiting. But these men have.

Ryder: Yeah . . . we've had enough of talking. Let's vote on it.

McLaughlin: No . . . it's out of the question. There's too much risk involved. We must learn how to . . . .

(Shouting from the crowd.)

Carroll: McLaughlin . . . we want to vote! You are the chairman of this committee. Call the vote.

McLaughlin: Please be patient.

(The crowd starts a slow handclap.)

Carroll: You know what they want, McLaughlin.

McLaughlin: I don't like it Carroll.

Carroll: I don't think you've got much choice.

McLaughlin: Very well. Silence, please. Silence. You all know the issue. All those in favour say "aye". *(A unanimous "aye")* All those against. *(There is silence)* They're all yours, Carroll.

Carroll: We must keep absolute secrecy, for one word in the wrong ear could ruin us. We shall meet here in three days at the same time, and I will tell you how it will be done . . . and when.

(From the very back of the stage voices can be heard. The men pick up their lanterns, leave the schoolroom, and join the backstage chorus.

All *(sing)*:
>Forty men went riding,
>Riding, riding.
>Forty men went riding
>Down the Roman line.

(Figures, dressed in black and muffled up, appear at the back of the set during the song. They have clubs and sticks. They circle the stage in sinister silhouettes)

>We met late in a schoolhouse
>Along the Roman line,
>Jim Carroll said, "Just wait, lads,
>'Til I give you the sign."
>With silent eyes we watched him,
>With clubs fixed in our hands.

Forty men went riding,
Riding, riding.
Forty men went riding
Down the Roman line.

(They fade into the shadows as Jim and Will enter. Slide 31 — night sky.)

Jim Donnelly: Are you sure you won't stop with us tonight, Will?

Will Donnelly: Not tonight. Big Charlie threw a shoe today. I've got to fix it by morning.

Jim Donnelly: Well, keep your eyes open when you ride home.

Will Donnelly: I always do, but it's a very quiet night. I was over at Keefe's Tavern earlier. You've never seen it so quiet.

Jim Donnelly: It's a strange day altogether. I was in town today, and there was scarce a man would look me in the eye. They look down at their feet and scuttle past, but when they think you're not looking, they stare at you. I don't like it. I wouldn't be surprised if Carroll and his cronies haven't been hatching a plot.

Will Donnelly: A plot? We've been living with a plot for forty years, father. It's no different today than it ever was.

Jim Donnelly: I don't know. There's a look in people's eyes different to what I've seen before.

Will Donnelly: It's just your imagination.

Jim Donnelly: Maybe. *(He shrugs)* Look at the sky, Will.

Will Donnelly: Clear. It's a grand night.

Jim Donnelly: Reminds me of the two years I spent on the run.

Will Donnelly: You still think about that?

Jim Donnelly: No. I hadn't thought about it in ages.

Will Donnelly: It must be a strange night if it gets you nostalgic. Is it because of the trial at Granton tomorrow?

Jim Donnelly: No . . . that doesn't worry me. There's not a scrap of evidence in that arson charge that isn't perjured. They'll never make it stick. What worries me is that most of our enemies are beginning to realize that their damned lies never hold water in court.

Will Donnelly: Why does that worry you?

Jim Donnelly: Because they may try something else.

Will Donnelly: Never. That bunch of gutless bastards would never have the nerve. You worry too much, father. By the way, do you want me to come over and look after the animals while you're away at Granton?

Jim Donnelly: Thank you, Will, but that young O'Connor boy is coming round to stay with us tonight.

Will Donnelly: Good. Well, the best of luck tomorrow. I'll see you after the trial.

Jim Donnelly: Right. Goodnight.

Will Donnelly: Goodnight.

(The vigilantes sing.)

All: Forty men went riding,
Riding, riding.
Forty men went riding
Down the Roman line.

(At the end of the song, the low, rumbling organ sound begins. The vigilantes move stealthily into their positions around the set. They wait, poised to spring. The centre of the stage becomes the living room of the Donnelly farm. It is empty. Carroll enters with a lantern. Slide 32 — cold colour — blue.)

Carroll *(calls out)*: Donnelly!

(There is a moment's silence, and Jim's voice is heard offstage.)

Jim Donnelly: Who is it?

Carroll: James Carroll. The constable.

(Jim comes onstage in his nightshirt. He is very sleepy.)

Jim Donnelly: What are you arresting me for now?

Carroll: I've got another charge against you.

(There is a silence while Jim, very annoyed, puts on his boots. Carroll sneaks up to another door and looks in. It is Tom Donnelly's bedroom. He enters and a moment later comes out, dragging behind him a drowsy Tom whom he has handcuffed.)

Tom Donnelly: What the hell?

Jim Donnelly: What's up, Tom? Are you handcuffed?

Tom Donnelly: Yes. He thinks he's smart.

(Jim snorts and heads for the bedroom.)

Carroll: Where do you think you're going?

Jim Donnelly: I'm going to get my coat.

(Carroll follows him to the bedroom door. Johannah enters.)

Johannah: What's going on?

Tom Donnelly: It's Carroll with another charge against us.

Johannah: Holy Jesus? Will we never have any peace? *(Shouts)* Bridget, get up and stoke the fire!

Jim Donnelly: Alright, Carroll . . . now read your warrant.

Carroll: There's plenty of time for that.

(Suddenly the vigilantes jump down from their positions. The organ sound has built into a powerful crescendo. There is a moment's pause — the vigilantes poised, the Donnellys shocked — then Carroll gives the first blow. Suddenly, everything is bedlam. Sticks and fists pounding, screams of terror and roars of rage. A movie projection appears on the screen. It is a collage of faces, the camera zooming in on expressions of fear and hatred. If slides are used, show actors faces in black and white. Slide 33 — faces. John Purtell chases Bridget up-

stairs with an axe. Bridget is followed by Johnny O'Connor, who has been in the bedroom of Jim Donnelly. As O'Connor reaches the top of the stairs, everything freezes. Irving appears at a higher level. Johnny O'Connor is about twelve years old.)

Irving: Johnny O'Connor. What were you doing in the early hours of February the fourth, 1880?

O'Connor: I was staying at the house of the Donnellys.

Irving: As the only surviving witness of the massacre, I hope you realize the importance of the accuracy of your testimony.

O'Connor: Yes, sir.

Irving: Who else was in the house that night?

O'Connor: There was Mr. and Mrs. Donnelly, and Tom and Bridget. Bridget was their niece, they said. Just come from Ireland.

Irving: You say that James Donnelly, Senior, went to the bedroom to get his coat, and you handed it to him?

O'Connor: Yes, sir.

Irving: Did you see anyone else?

O'Connor: I saw James Carroll, the constable, standing in the doorway.

Irving: What happened after the other men entered?

O'Connor: I ran to the top of the stairs after Bridget Donnelly, but she closed the door in my face, so I ran downstairs and hid under the bed.

Irving: Did you recognize any of the men?

O'Connor: Yes, sir.

Irving: What happened next?

O'Connor: Someone smashed the light. It was difficult to see.

(There is the sound of breaking glass and the scene dims, so that only

shadows can be seen. Chaos suddenly bursts out again. The movie or slide collage starts again — similar to the first. John Purtell runs up the stairs and grabs Bridget who is screaming with fear. He has an axe.)

Purtell: You bitch! I'm going to slash you to pieces, you bitch!

(Tom Donnelly manages to chop his way through the oncoming crowd and knocks several of them down. He reaches the door and forces his way outside. Several men follow him. Bridget has been dragged down the stairs, and John Purtell smashes her with his axe, screaming like a maniac. Meanwhile, Jim and Johannah are being clubbed in a corner. Jim is the first to fall. They turn their attention to Johannah. One of them grabs a red hot poker and the others hold Johannah down.)

Ryder: Let's hear the bitch sizzle!

(He rams the poker up her crotch, and she screams terribly. They throw her on the floor and continue to club her. Tom is dragged in by several men. This can be a dummy made to resemble the actor playing Tom so that he can be decapitated. He is beaten up and bloody. Finally, he is thrown on the floor. A man is poised with a spade. Everybody freezes.)

Irving: What was the last thing that happened during the fight?

O'Connor: Tom was the last to die, I think. They were doing terrible things to him. They chopped his head off with a spade.

(The spade comes down on Tom's head with a thump and decapitates him. The body twitches, and then is still. The movie or slide projection fades into blood running down a white background. There is silence, except for the heavy breathing of the vigilantes. As they survey the scene of their night's work, a feeling of horror and disgust begins to run through the group. Carroll senses it . . . .)

Carroll: Don't just stand there, for chrissake! We have work to do. Who has the oil?

Madigan *(still shocked)*: It's here.

Carroll: Get on with it then. Burn this place to the ground! Come on . . . move! *(Madigan throws the oil around and simulates setting it alight. A lot of the group are still stunned)* We're going to Will

Dudley Witn[ey]

Donnelly's next, and I'll beat the hell out of anyone who plays chicken on me now. Let's get out of here. *(The men pull themselves together and leave as the music begins. The music is the theme of "Forty Men Went Riding". The bodies still remain on the stage, as the stage fills with smoke and the sound of flames. This fades as if receding into the distance, and the scene becomes moonlight outside Will Donnelly's house. The vigilantes poise on one side of the stage, three rifles aimed at a door. Carroll shouts —)* Fire . . . fire! *(Silence)* Open up! There's a fire!

(A light appears in a window. Slowly the door opens and a figure is silhouetted in the doorway.)

John Donnelly: What do you . . . .

(Three guns go off. He goes flying backwards and collapses.)

Man 1: We've got him, boys, we've got him!

McLaughlin: Come on, let's go. Our work is done.

(The vigilantes exit and Will Donnelly comes running out.)

Will Donnelly: My God! It's John! They've killed my brother!

(They freeze. Suddenly, there is a loud hammering. It is Johnny O'Connor at the Whalen's house. This scene takes place in a separate area so that the bodies can remain on stage. A light goes on and Mrs. Whalen appears. The hammering is quite frantic. Slide 34 — red.)

Mrs. Whalen: Who is it?

O'Connor: It's Johnny O'Connor.

Mr. Whalen *(entering)*: What's the matter?

Mrs. Whalen: It's the O'Connor boy.

Mr. Whalen: What are you doing up at this hour?

O'Connor: I'm froze, Mr. Whalen.

Mrs. Whalen: Where on earth are your shoes?

O'Connor: I had to leave them at the Donnelly's. Don't you have a coat or something? I'm frozen.

Mr. Whalen: What do you mean you had to leave them at the Donnellys? What happened?

O'Connor: The Donnelly house is on fire.

Mr. Whalen: You're dreaming, boy.

O'Connor: A lot of men came in and beat them up with sticks. I think they're all killed.

Mr. Whalen: They're what?

Mrs. Whalen: Do you know what you're saying boy?

O'Connor: They're all killed and Carroll the constable was there.

(Mr. and Mrs. Whalen look at each other.)

Mrs. Whalen: Now you don't say anything more about it. We don't want to be brought into this.

Mr. Whalen: The missus is right, boy. You'd better be mighty careful of what you say. They'll be dragging you in front of a court if something really has happened.

O'Connor: Well, go over and see. Call up your boys and tell them to put the fire out.

Mrs. Whalen: I don't like the sound of this. You say Carroll was there boy?

O'Connor: That's right. And I saw Ryder and Purtell, as well.

Mrs. Whalen: The committee was out tonight.

(Mr. Whalen grabs Johnny O'Connor.)

Mr. Whalen: What happened? What did they do?

O'Connor: They killed them all, Tom and Bridget and Mrs. Donnelly and the old man. They're all dead.

Mr. Whalen *(looks out)*: Holy Christ! It's done at last!

(They exit. The bodies of the four Donnellys killed at the farm are lying downstage in the same positions as when they were murdered, and the body of John Donnelly with Will is in the same position as at the end of the earlier scene. During the song Will moves in among the dead bodies and looks at them. Standing around the stage are the men of the vigilante committee. They are facing the audience.)

All *(sing)*:
> We're only honest farmers
> And we've no mind to kill,
> But if our homes are threatened
> Then, by Christ, we will.
>
> A brighter dawn is breaking
> Though red has tinged the sky.
> We've left our hate behind us
> Where crimson ashes lie.

(Sound effect like alarm bell indicates sudden clamour and confusion. Rushing everywhere on stage are reporters, frantically asking questions. During this, newspaper vendors rush on shouting the headlines. Men begin to take the bodies off on stretchers. Mulligan enters and looks around to see what is going on. Slide 35 — newspaper.)

Vendor 1: Biddulph horror! Family massacred!

(Slide 36 — newspaper.)

Vendor 2: Horrible tragedy at Lucan! Result of a family feud!

Vendor 3: Family who terrorized district, murdered by neighbours!

(Slide 37 — newspaper.)

Reporter 1: I'm from the London Free Press. Can you tell me about this feud?

Man 1: Feud? What feud?

(Slide 38 — newspaper.)

Reporter 2: I'm from the Toronto Globe. Did you know the Donnellys?

Mulligan: Well, Tom was about seven feet tall and just about as broad If he didn't like a man's looks, he'd change them — permanently.

(Slide 39 — newspaper.)

Reporter 3: London Advertiser. Who do you think did the killing?

Man 3: If it were known, it will be found that the murderers are the most respectable men in the township, good farmers and honest men. But they had to do it — there was no other way.

(Slide 40 — neutral colour — green. At a higher level there is a burst of riotous laughter, and a light comes up to reveal McLaughlin, Ryder and three other men blind drunk. During this scene, the last of the bodies are removed slowly. McLaughlin is stunned and doesn't join in the celebration. The other men sing "Honest Farmers", but raucously out of tune.)

Men: We're only honest farmers
And we've no mind to kill
But if our homes are threatened
Then, by Christ, we will.

Ryder: Did you see how they got the old woman? *(Laughs)* With a poker up her . . . . *(Indicates it.)*

(Everyone laughs.)

Purtell: Did you hear that there weren't enough of the bodies left after the burning, so they put them all in one coffin. *(The others laugh)* That's right . . . the old man, the old woman, Tom and Bridget . . . all in one coffin. *(More laughter)* And John had one all to himself

Ryder: Listen to this, everybody! "There does not appear to be much sympathy for the murdered family, on account of the strong feeling that existed against them."

Toohey: You think that's good? How about this one? "Little can be heard in condemnation of the murderers, while such expressions as, 'It's about time they were cleaned out' can be heard by many of the townsfolk." *(They laugh)* We'll be heroes yet!

Purtell: Did you see how Jim here cut Tom's head off with a spade?

(They all laugh) He couldn't find his axe, so the silly bugger used a spade!

(They laugh at him again.)

Ryder: We oughta call him "Spadey".

(They all applaud and bang their glasses on the table shouting, "Spadey, Spadey.")

Toohey: I've got a good one from the Globe in Toronto: "The Donnellys had the unenviable reputation of being the terrors of the township."

Ryder *(splitting himself with laughter)*: Terrors of the township! Oh . . . that's a good one. *(They both rock with laughter. Ryder gets up with difficulty)* I propose a toast. Fill her up. *(The glasses are filled)* I propose a toast to those dear departed friends who cannot be with us today. The terrors of this township!

McLaughlin: Long live the terrors of the township!

(They burst into laughter again and drink their toast. Ryder drains his bottle.)

Ryder: Come on, boys . . . let's get some more whisky. *(They move down from their higher level to centre stage, from which the bodies have been removed. A man enters)* Josh . . . a great night for a celebration! *(The man turns his back on them and stands motionless. A lady enters)* Good evening to you, Beth. *(She turns her back on them)* For chrissake! We're only drunk. *(Four more people enter and turn away from them — all remaining motionless on stage)* Talk to us, you bastards! Ah . . . to hell with you all. Let's go down to Keefe's Tavern.

(They exit. Will and Mulligan are still in the background.)

Will Donnelly: Mulligan! At the Central Hotel last week, you were heard saying you saw a meeting of the vigilante committee. Who did you see there?

One: I saw nothing.

Two: I heard nothing.

Three: I know nothing.

Four: I saw nothing.

Five: I heard nothing.

Six: I know nothing.

Will Donnelly: You must have seen something. Something that can be used as evidence.

Mulligan: There's nothing I can tell you, Will. I'm sorry, but . . . .

One: I saw nothing.

Two: I heard nothing.

Three: I know nothing.

Four: I saw nothing.

Five: I heard nothing.

Six: I know nothing.

Will Donnelly: Why won't you help me . . . why the hell won't anybody help me?

Mulligan: I can't help you. Nobody can help. All you got left is the law! Good luck!

(Slide 41 — inside church. There is a silence and the Kyrie begins. During the Kyrie, the congregation files in and two coffins are carried to centre stage. Father Connolly is on a higher level, as if in a pulpit.)

Father Connolly: I urge you all to pray for the souls of the departed, and I feel certain that this most dreadful act had been the result of midnight walking, drinking and carousing.

(A light falls on Irving, changing the pulpit to the witness box.)

Irving: Father Connolly, why did you instigate the vigilance committee?

Father Connolly: I did not instigate it. It was already in existence

Irving: But you proposed the signing of an oath.

Father Connolly: It was my intention to make sure that its activities were beneficial.

Irving: Did you mean by that the elimination of the Donnellys?

Father Connolly: No, sir. I did not.

Irving: And yet you asked your parishioners to, and I quote, "solemnl pledge ourselves to aid our spiritual director and parish priest in the discovery and putting down of crime in our mission."

Father Connolly: I did not mention the Donnellys.

Irving: And yet you are said to have cursed them from the pulpit.

Father Connolly: That is not true.

Irving: But you did speak out against them.

Father Connolly: I never mentioned them by name.

Irving: It is said that you refused to confess John Donnelly, not long before his death.

Father Connolly: I refused to confess him, because I thought that he intended to confess to an untruth, in order to free his brother and implicate others.

Irving: Don't you think that this is a rather presumptuous attitude for a priest? *(Father Connolly is silent)* What did he do when you told him that?

Father Connolly: He went away.

Irving: So you sent him to his death unshriven?

Father Connolly: But I never meant . . . I never meant it to be like this . . . . *(The light fades on Irving, and Father Connolly is back in the pulpit. A bell tolls)* Today is one of the saddest days of my life. Here are the last earthly remains of five souls whose deaths at the hands of murderers have been a great shock to us all. *(He is overcome with emotion)* A great shock. It may be said that I was not in friendship with the family. That is not true. I was in friendship with the old people, but the young people I did not know much. Particularly with the old woman I was friendly. For two hours she was in my office on Christmas eve giving me the history of her whole life in Biddulph. She received the sacrament, and the last words she spoke to me as she went away were, "Father Connolly, I am going to get not only my boys, but all the Biddulph boys to reform." Who would have thought it would have come to this! *(Silence)* I can't say any more.

(The scene freezes in a tableau. A light comes up on Tim Mulligan. Slide 42 — a cold colour — blue.)

Mulligan: A pretty little picture, isn't it? Father Connolly bawling his eyes out on the coffins. The good citizens of Biddulph sitting quietly through the whole thing, with their hands clenched in prayer and their hearts clenched in hate. There was more than a few in that house of God that day wishing them eternal torment between the lines of the Lord's Prayer. And, of course, Will — his face straight and unmoved. I don't know a man ever saw him smile after the murder — or show anything, come to that. Revenge was all he wanted, but now it was him who had to fight with the tangled web of the law. He wasn't used to fighting that way. Poor bastard. And so there came the trial — for all that it was worth.

Judge: The jury will now retire to consider its verdict.

All *(sing)*:
>The words have all been spoken,
>Our story's almost done.
>But the legend of the Donnellys
>Has only just begun.
>
>But the facts are soon forgotten
>As you watch a legend grow,
>And the truth of all that happened
>I guess we'll never know.

Judge: How do you find the defendants on the charge of murder?

Foreman: Not guilty, Your Honour.

(The band begins a slow, sombre introduction to "Months Are Going".)

All *(sing)*:
>Months are going, going by,
>Wheat is growing, growing high,
>But someone soon is going to die,
>Way down in Lucan town.

Will Donnelly: The work of a lifetime. Memories crumbled in ashes that blow and settle on the snow. Soon they will be lost to the earth, lost in the land they created and that created them. It's all over. I'm too tired to fight any more.

(He breaks down and exits.)

All *(sing)*:
>The words have all been spoken
>Our story's almost done.
>But the legend of the Donnellys
>Has only just begun.
>
>Kids huddle by the fireside
>Amid a winter's gale,
>And grand-folks talk in whispered tones
>About this fearful tale.
>
>And mothers tell their children
>To bolt their windows tight,
>For the Devil and the Donnellys
>Are riding past tonight.
>
>For the facts are soon forgotten
>As you watch a legend grow.
>And the truth of all that happened
>I guess we'll never know.
>
>Follow us . . . one hundred years,
>And we'll take you back to Lucan town . . . .

(The final line is incomplete and the sound of a man whistling takes over. The accompanying music fades away just leaving the whistling alone. Meanwhile, a movie projection appears. It is the same as the opening sequence, except that Will is walking away from the camera.

By the time the whistling ends, Will is far away on the skyline. The sound of an icy winter wind takes over from the whistling, as the movie fades out leaving only darkness and the sound of the wind. Alternatively, the silhouette of Will Donnelly can walk in front of the screen, then exit. Curtain.)

The end

Photo credits A1 *(The Company)*
(left to right) A16 *(Karna Ivey, Diane Cuthbert)*
A39 *(Robert Cooper, Greg Brandt, Peter Colley, David G. Marriage, Art Fidler, Tom Stebing, David Wasse, Claude R. Tessier, Tim Grantham, Cecil Wilson)*
A50 *(Tom Celli, Peter Colley)*
A70 *(Art Fidler, David Wallett, Cecil Wilson, Jim Schaefer, Tom Stebing, Rick Prevett)*
A75 *(David Wallett, Cecil Wilson)*
A89 *(Pat Collins, Tom Celli)*
A92 *(The Company)*
A107 *(Jim Schaefer, Tom Celli)*

Photographs by Jim Hockings.

Additional credits A8, A54, A61, A64, A84, A96, A102 *(Courtesy of the Picture Collection, Fine Arts Department, Metropolitan Toronto Central Library, Toronto, Ontario)*

A24–A25, A31, A45, A81 *(Courtesy of the Historical Atlas of Middlesex County, Ontario, as compiled by H.R.Page and Company, Toronto, Ontario, in 1878. It was edited by Mika Silk Screening Limited of Belleville, Ontario, and printed by Maracle Press, Oshawa, Ontario, in 1972)*

Sources of research material

The author wishes to acknowledge the following sources for his research into the Donnelly family:

"The Donnellys Must Die" by Orlo Miller; published by Macmillan Company of Canada Limited, Toronto, Ontario.

"The Black Donnellys (The True Story of Canada's Most Barbaric Feud)" by Thomas P. Kelley; published by Modern Canadian Library Ink, Toronto, Ontario.

"The London Free Press", London, Ontario.

"The Globe", Toronto, Ontario.

Various legal documents of the period.

Original music

Original music composed for THE DONNELLYS is available from Berthold Carrière, c/o Simon & Pierre Publishing Company Limited, Toronto, Ontario.

Technical effects

A combination of sound tapes, slides and film projections was used in the original production. Sound effects and slides are available on a rental basis from Simon & Pierre Publishing Company Limited, Toronto. The film projections can be omitted if desired, but were used by Theatre London to heighten certain dramatic moments.

Projection one — at the opening of the play as described in the text.

Projection two — a burning barn in the sequence with Toohey and his family in Act one.

Projection three — a collage of faces during the massacre in Act two.

Projection four — blood running down a white screen after Tom's head is severed in Act two.

Projection five: — at the closing of the play as described in the text.

Costumes

There were really no definable costumes. Everyone wore a basic black outfit and various nondescript hats and jackets were added. Mulligan had a large, dirty trench coat.

Set design The design for the original production of THE DONNELLYS, as shown opposite, used a series of ramps and risers. This created a variety of levels in staging, as well as flexibility and speed in scene changing. The numbers 1 to 13 indicate thirteen detachable masking pieces.

Props *The following props were used in the original production, although not all are mentioned in the text.*

Shawls	Bundles
Aprons	Stools
Assorted jackets	Barrel
Petition	Wash basket
Pencil	Harness
Warrants	Butter churn
Newspapers	Tray
Oath	Beer mugs
Land deed	Mulligan's whisky bottle
Paper	Jugs
Pen	Lanterns
Ink	Handcuffs
Axes	Oil can
File	Logs
Rope	Planks
Mallets	Thorns
Spades	Stretchers
Fake spade	Blanket
Fake hatchet	Two coffins
Soft clubs	Mulligan's knapsack
Two revolvers	Luggage
Shot gun	Trunks
Poker	Fire bell
Cane	Funeral bell
Handspike	Dummy
Manacles	Baby

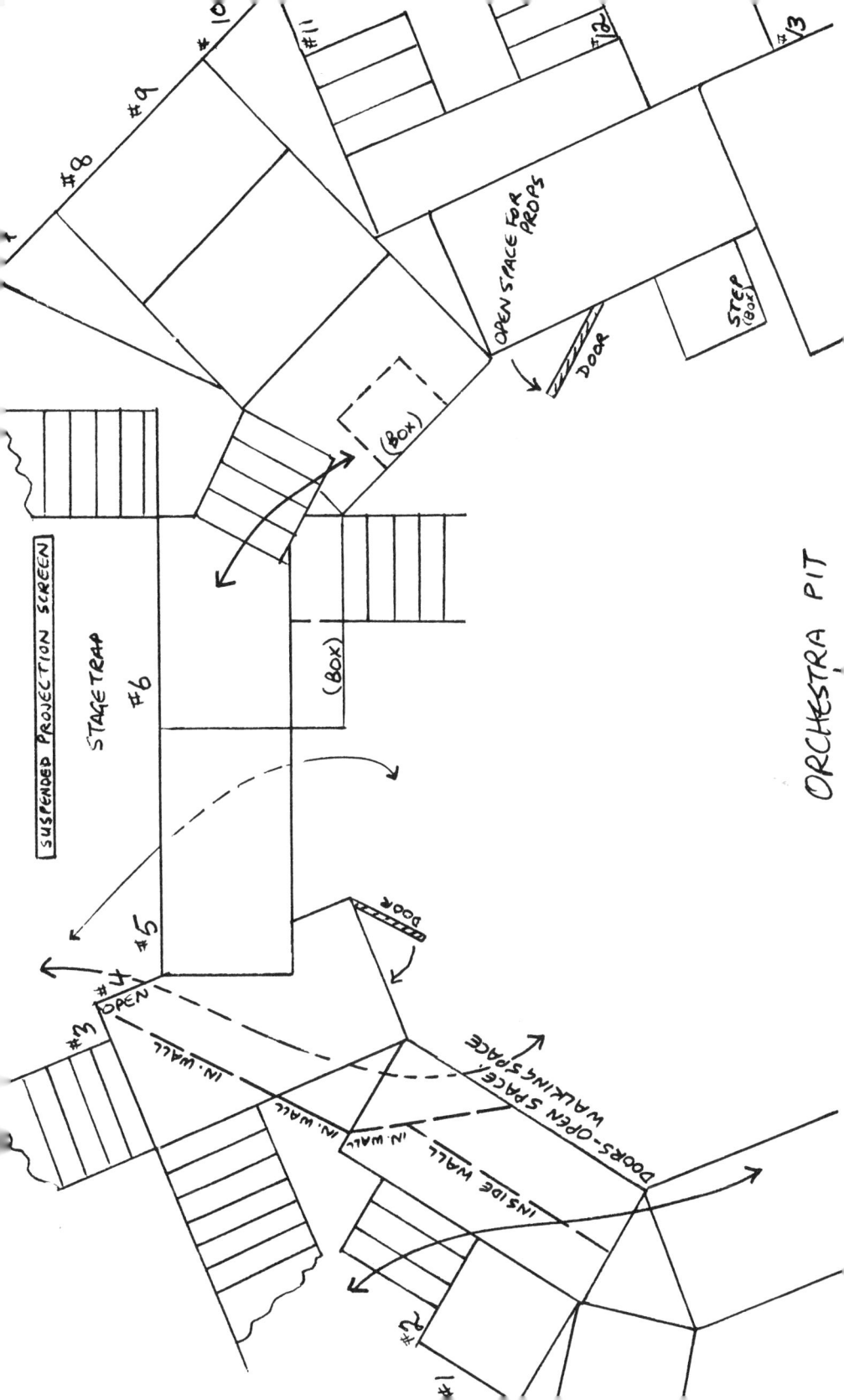